Where to Stand

Finding Solid Ground in a Shifting World

James J. Burke

Fireproof Commentaries

FIREPROOF
COMMENTARIES

ISBN-13: 979-8-9941637-9-5

All Scripture quotations are taken from the King
James Version of the Bible unless otherwise
indicated.

Printed in the United States of America
fireproofcommentaries.org

Table of Contents

Preface

Standing on What Holds

Most people do not spend their lives asking whether they believe in God. They are far more concerned with whether life itself can be trusted—whether it will hold under pressure, whether it makes sense of joy and suffering, whether it offers anything solid enough to stand on.

We build our lives on explanations. Some are inherited, some are assembled over time, and others are adopted simply because they seem to work. We trust ideas about progress, identity, freedom, goodness, and success to give our lives stability. Yet many discover—sometimes slowly, sometimes suddenly—that these explanations do not bear weight. Anxiety increases. Meaning feels fragile. Guilt resurfaces no matter how carefully it is buried. What once felt firm begins to shift.

This book begins with a simple observation: much of modern life is spent trying to stand on ground that was never meant to hold us.

The Bible often speaks of foundations, ground, and rock, not as poetic decoration, but as descriptions of reality. Some ground shifts. Some ground absorbs effort but produces nothing. Some ground hides what we would rather forget, only to uncover it again later. Other ground is solid—capable of bearing weight, sustaining life, and enduring exposure.

Jesus once described human life in these terms. One person builds on sand, another on rock. Both build. Both hope. Both intend permanence. The difference is not effort or sincerity, but whether the ground beneath them can hold.

That image is often reduced to a warning about storms. But the problem is deeper than crisis. Sand does not only fail when trouble comes; it fails every day. It shifts with the wind. It resists growth. It intrudes everywhere. It obscures vision. Life lived on sand requires constant adjustment just to remain upright, and even then, nothing truly settles.

Rock is different. Rock holds. Rock anchors. Rock allows soil to gather, roots to take hold, and life to grow. Rock bears weight without collapse and remains steady long after surface conditions change.

This book argues that the Christian message—what the Bible calls salvation—is not primarily about emotional comfort, moral improvement, or religious belonging. It is about where a person stands. Salvation is not merely rescue from a moment of danger; it is relocation from unstable ground to solid footing. It is being placed where truth, justice, forgiveness, and hope can finally rest without sinking.

That claim carries serious implications. If there is such a thing as solid ground, then not all explanations of life are equally reliable. If there is a foundation that holds, then some of what we trust now must be provisional at best—and deceptive at worst. And if Jesus Christ is that foundation, then He is not merely a spiritual option among many, but the underlying reality upon which life was always meant to stand.

The purpose of this book is not to pressure belief, manipulate emotion, or win arguments. Its aim is clarity. It seeks to examine the ground we currently trust, to test whether it can bear the weight we place upon it, and to present Jesus Christ as He is—not as an abstract idea or moral teacher, but as the Rock revealed beneath the sand.

The chapters that follow move deliberately. They begin with shared human experience: instability, moral tension, and the sense that something is not holding. They then turn to the person and work of Christ—His incarnation, His death, and His resurrection—as decisive acts that secure a foundation capable of bearing reality itself. Finally, they consider what it means to step off collapsing ground and stand where life can grow.

Nothing in this book requires prior theological training. But it does require honesty—about the weight life places on us, and about whether what we trust can truly support it.

If you have ever felt that the explanations you rely on keep shifting beneath your feet, this book is written for you. Not to offer a mirage of stability, but to point you toward ground that holds.

This book does not begin by asking you to believe—but by asking whether what you trust can actually hold you.

James J. Burke

Marinette, Wisconsin

January, 2026

Where to Stand

I

Life in the Sand

1

Who Are You?

It Depends Who's Asking

Ask someone today, "Who are you?" and the honest answer is often, "Which version?"

The answer changes depending on the room, the crowd, the platform, or the moment. At work, one identity is emphasized—competent, agreeable, careful. Online, another—opinionated, principled, curated. Among friends, a different one still—relaxed, ironic, selectively honest. Certain parts of the self are highlighted, others carefully hidden.

This isn't dishonesty. It's survival.

Large numbers of people now admit openly that they do not feel free to speak their minds, not because of legal consequences, but because of social ones.[1]

Many have learned—through experience rather than theory—that saying the wrong thing can cost relationships, reputation, or opportunity. Silence often feels safer than honesty.

A person quickly learns that the same sentence can sound acceptable in one setting and dangerous in another. A joke that lands with friends would be risky at work. An opinion shared online might need to be softened—or deleted—before a family gathering. Silence in one space is wisdom; in another, it is read as hostility.

Identity has become situational. What once felt like authenticity now feels conditional—something that must be managed rather than expressed.

Living Inside a Sorting System

Modern society is organized around identity categories.

Race, sexuality, gender expression, political persuasion, education, income, trauma, hobbies, fandoms, moral stances—each functions as a sorting mechanism. These labels are treated as explanatory: this is who you are, therefore this is how you think, vote, behave, and belong.

In professional environments, this pressure becomes especially visible. A majority of workers report that they actively "cover"—downplaying or concealing parts of who they are—in order to fit in.[2] They learn which opinions are safe, which stories are best left untold, and which parts of themselves might quietly complicate advancement or acceptance.

Even leisure becomes diagnostic. What you watch, play, read, or follow is treated as a signal. A credential may grant authority in one space and suspicion in another. A personal story of suffering may earn sympathy—or be dismissed as insufficient compared to someone else's.

The problem is not that these things are meaningless. The problem is that none of them are stable enough to carry the full weight being placed upon them.

They overlap. They conflict. Their meanings shift. What grants acceptance in one space can provoke rejection in another. What once secured belonging can later invite scrutiny or exclusion.

So identity must be constantly recalculated.

Middle School Never Ended

For many adults, this produces a familiar feeling—one most people thought they had left behind.

Life begins to feel like middle school with adult consequences.

Social groups form and dissolve. Language changes quickly. Status is fragile. People learn to scan conversations before entering them, to measure how far they can speak before needing to qualify or retreat. Those who don't fully fit within a single ideological or social "bundle" often feel the pressure most intensely, discovering that partial agreement is no longer enough to secure belonging.[3]

Nuance becomes risky. Independence becomes lonely.

Being on the wrong side of a disagreement—or even silent at the wrong moment—can cost social standing, professional opportunity, or relational access. Everyone is watching everyone else, and no one is quite sure what the rules are anymore.

The stakes are higher now, but the dynamics are the same. Belonging is provisional. Identity is public. Mistakes are remembered and reinterpreted.

This is not immaturity. It is what happens when identity is treated as social currency rather than something grounded.

When Identity Has No Weight

The deeper problem is not that identity matters too much, but that it is being asked to carry more weight than it can hold.

Identity is now expected to do the work once done by family, faith, tradition, vocation, and community. It must explain who you are, justify why you belong, defend your moral standing, and protect you from judgment—all at once.

That is an impossible load.

When identity is built on social recognition, it feels solid only as long as recognition lasts. Approval provides temporary support, but it cannot bear pressure. The moment that approval wavers—or turns—the ground beneath identity gives way.

This is why so many people feel anxious even when they are affirmed.

Affirmed, but Still Afraid

Affirmation was never designed to carry identity.

It feels stabilizing at first. Being seen, validated, or included brings relief. But relief fades quickly, because affirmation depends on continued alignment. It must be renewed. It must be maintained. It can be withdrawn.

People sense this intuitively.

A person who is affirmed today wonders what will be required tomorrow. Will the same language still be acceptable? Will the same stance still be praised? Will yesterday's ally become today's critic?

So affirmation becomes something to manage rather than enjoy. Identity remains light, brittle, easily shaken.

Identity Under Pressure

Pressure exposes weight limits.

A professional setback, a public disagreement, a personal failure—these moments reveal whether identity can hold. For many, identity collapses not because they lack sincerity, but because what they were standing on was never meant to bear strain.

A label that once felt empowering now feels confining. A group that once offered belonging now demands conformity. A narrative that once explained everything now requires constant revision.

When identity is challenged, people instinctively rush to defend it—not because they are proud, but because collapse feels imminent.

Identity without weight cannot absorb shock.

Why Guilt Breaks Through

This is also why guilt behaves so stubbornly in modern life.

When identity is fragile, guilt becomes dangerous. It threatens not just behavior, but belonging. So it must be minimized, reframed, or redirected as quickly as possible.

People learn to explain themselves before being asked. They preemptively qualify statements. They compare themselves to worse examples. They insist on context—not always dishonestly, but desperately.

Yet guilt has a way of resurfacing.

A memory intrudes. A pattern repeats. A failure contradicts the story being told. And because identity is already under strain, guilt feels heavier than it should.

It isn't heavier.

The ground is lighter.

Justice Without Resolution

The same lack of weight affects justice.

Outrage feels intense because it is carrying more than it should. It is expected to secure moral standing, restore balance, and signal belonging—all at once. But outrage cannot resolve what identity cannot carry.

So justice becomes performative. Statements are made. Positions are declared. But nothing settles. The sense of moral imbalance remains.

People care deeply about justice while quietly suspecting that it never truly arrives.

Identity cannot hold what justice requires.

The Quiet Fear Beneath It All

Beneath the public language of identity lies a quieter fear: What if this doesn't hold when it matters most?

This fear does not belong only to those on the margins. It belongs equally to those at the center. In fact, it often intensifies with status, visibility, or influence, because there is more to lose.

Identity that depends on recognition must always be defended.

And anything that must always be defended is already unstable.

The Question Beneath the Labels

This is why so many people feel anxious even when they are accepted, and defensive even when they are affirmed.

They sense something is wrong, but they can't quite name it.

The problem is not that identity is important.

The problem is that identity has been placed on ground that cannot hold it.

So before asking who you are, a more basic question must be answered:

What are you standing on?

Because until the ground is solid, no identity can be stable.

Why Identity Is So Hard to Hold

Identity was never meant to be generated from within.

Human beings discover who they are in relationship— through belonging, recognition, and continuity over time. Identity forms where there is stability: shared language, shared expectations, shared memory.

But when those structures weaken, identity becomes difficult not because people are confused, but because the conditions required for identity formation are missing.

Today, the social signposts that once helped people locate themselves are shifting constantly. Language changes quickly. Moral expectations evolve unevenly. Communities fragment and re-form. Connections are stressed by mobility, technology, and distrust.

The result is not freedom, but uncertainty.

People are told to "be themselves" at the very moment when there is no stable reference for what that means. They are encouraged to construct identity from the inside while the outside world continually redefines what will be recognized or rejected.

This creates an impossible task.

Identity Without Anchors

When identity must be generated internally, it becomes fragile.

A person can know what they feel today and doubt it tomorrow. They can believe something sincerely and be told it is outdated or harmful. They can commit to a role, a community, or a cause—only to find that its meaning has shifted underneath them.

Without shared anchors, identity becomes provisional. It holds only until the environment changes.

This is why identity feels exhausting rather than empowering. It must be continually reinforced because nothing outside the self confirms it for long.

Connection Under Strain

At the same time, relationships—the very places where identity once stabilized—are under strain

People move more often. Communities are thinner. Trust is fragile. Disagreement feels dangerous. Social interaction is increasingly mediated and public.

This makes identity both more visible and more vulnerable.

People are expected to present a coherent self while navigating fractured connections. They must maintain identity without the support systems that once made identity possible.

The result is not self-knowledge, but anxiety.

Why This Matters

This difficulty is not a personal failure. It is a structural problem.

Identity cannot be sustained where belonging is conditional and recognition is unstable. Asking people to build themselves in such conditions is like asking them to build on sand while the wind keeps changing direction.

Until there is stable ground beneath identity, identity will remain difficult to hold—no matter how sincere the effort.

When Nothing Fully Settles

When identity must be constantly managed, life begins to feel unsettled even when nothing is obviously wrong.

On the surface, things may appear stable. Work continues. Relationships function. Daily routines hold. But beneath that surface, there is a persistent sense that nothing quite lands. Decisions feel provisional. Convictions feel temporary. Confidence fades quickly and must be reinforced again and again.

People often describe this feeling as anxiety or restlessness, but those words don't quite capture it. It is less a spike of fear and more a low-grade instability —a sense that life requires constant adjustment just to remain upright.

Nothing ever fully settles.

The Subtle Instability of Everyday Life

This instability shows up in small, ordinary ways.

People replay conversations long after they end, wondering how they were perceived. They hesitate before speaking, weighing not just whether something is true, but how it might be interpreted. They soften statements, add disclaimers, or avoid topics altogether—not because they have nothing to say, but because saying the wrong thing feels costly.

Even success brings unease. A promotion raises new expectations. Recognition creates pressure to remain consistent. Being seen increases vulnerability. Relief never quite becomes rest.

Identity that depends on shifting recognition cannot relax.

Confidence That Requires Maintenance

When nothing settles, confidence becomes something that must be maintained rather than enjoyed.

People feel confident only while things are going well —while affirmation continues, alignment holds, and approval remains intact. The moment conditions change, confidence drains away.

So energy is spent maintaining alignment: staying current with language, tracking social cues, monitoring reactions. The self is continually adjusted to remain acceptable.

This is not vanity. It is what happens when identity is unsupported.

Meaning That Must Be Rebuilt

Instability also affects meaning.

People speak about purpose and values with sincerity, but those meanings feel vulnerable to disruption. A moral failure, a public conflict, or a personal loss can unravel narratives that once felt secure.

Meaning must then be rebuilt—sometimes repeatedly.

What once felt like a stable sense of self begins to feel like a story that must be retold carefully, with edits and explanations, to remain credible. Over time, the effort required to sustain meaning becomes heavier than meaning itself.

Rest That Never Quite Arrives

One of the clearest signs that nothing has settled is the absence of real rest.

People may stop working, but they do not feel rested. They may disconnect briefly, but the underlying tension remains. Time off becomes recovery rather than renewal.

Rest feels undeserved, unsafe, or temporary—something that must be justified or limited. Even moments of quiet carry a subtle pressure to prepare for what comes next.

Stable ground allows rest. Unstable ground does not.

Why This Feels Normal

Many people do not recognize this condition as instability because it has become common.

When constant adjustment is required, adjustment feels normal. When vigilance is expected, vigilance feels responsible. When rest feels risky, exhaustion can even feel mature.

In a world that rewards adaptability, the ability to stay upright under strain is praised. People learn to treat unease as the price of awareness and fatigue as the cost of being thoughtful.

But what is common is not always healthy. And what feels normal is not always sustainable.

Life was not meant to require this much effort just to stand.

The Accumulation of Weight

Instability rarely announces itself all at once. It accumulates.

Small stresses add up. Minor anxieties compound. Guilt resurfaces. Questions about justice linger without resolution. The sense of carrying something uncertain grows heavier over time—not because circumstances necessarily worsen, but because nothing ever absorbs the weight.

Eventually, many people reach a point of quiet exhaustion. Not collapse, but fatigue. They are tired of managing. Tired of explaining. Tired of holding everything together.

They are tired of standing on something that will not hold still.

Stability That Requires Constant Effort

Much of modern life is organized around adaptability. Flexibility is praised. Fluidity is treated as wisdom. Commitments are kept light. Options are kept open. Identity itself is framed as something to be continually revised.

Beneath this way of thinking is a quiet assumption: if life feels unstable, it is because we have not adapted well enough.

So the solution is always more effort—better strategies, sharper self-awareness, improved control. We are told to recalibrate, reframe, optimize.

But stability that requires constant effort is not stability.

It is balance under strain.

When the ground beneath us is firm, effort produces growth. When the ground is unstable, effort is consumed simply staying upright. Energy that might have been spent building a life is spent preventing collapse.

Over time, this produces exhaustion rather than fulfillment.

Many people adjust to this without ever naming it. They lower expectations. They redefine success. They learn not to hope too much. These adjustments can feel wise—even mature—but they often come at a quiet cost: the loss of confidence that life itself can be trusted.

Explanations That Shift Under Weight

Every life rests on explanations.

We rely on ideas—sometimes unexamined ones—to tell us who we are, what matters, and how to make sense of suffering and joy. These explanations form the ground on which we stand.

Some explanations work reasonably well until they are tested. Meaning built on achievement can hold while success lasts, but it weakens under failure. Identity built on self-expression can feel liberating, but it offers little protection when desires conflict or change. Moral systems grounded in consensus work until injustice demands more than agreement.

The test is not whether an explanation sounds convincing.

It is whether it can bear weight.

Weight comes in many forms: guilt that cannot be dismissed, suffering that cannot be explained away, injustice that demands judgment, love that risks loss. When these pressures arrive, shifting explanations reveal their limits. They rarely collapse all at once. They erode. They soften. They retreat into ambiguity.

What often follows is not disbelief, but improvisation. New explanations are layered over old ones. Language becomes more flexible, less precise. The ground continues to shift, but we learn to move with it.

When Language Loses Its Ground

One of the clearest signs that the ground is shifting is a change in language.

Words that once assumed fixed meaning are replaced with words that allow negotiation. This usually happens quietly—through small adjustments that feel reasonable at the time.

Consider the difference between virtue and value.

Virtue assumes a standard beyond the individual. To speak of virtue is to acknowledge that some things are right or wrong regardless of preference. Virtue belongs to solid ground.

Value, by contrast, speaks of relative worth. Values are held, prioritized, revised, and exchanged. Everyone has values. Not everyone recognizes virtue. A culture built on values alone has no stable reference point by which to judge them.

This shift matters. When moral language moves from virtue to value, standards are not denied—they are softened. Judgment is not rejected—it is deferred. Moral seriousness remains, but moral ground erodes.

Missionary Don Richardson once described a culture that admired treachery and deceit. In that society, betrayal was celebrated rather than condemned. By the logic of values alone, such a system is as valid as any other. Only an external standard makes judgment possible.

This is how instability spreads—not through open rejection of morality, but through language that preserves moral feeling while quietly removing moral ground.

What the Ground Cannot Hold

Shifting ground fails in predictable ways.

It cannot sustain justice, because justice requires standards that do not change when they become inconvenient. It cannot absorb guilt, because guilt is weight, not feeling—it can be buried for a time, but it resurfaces. It cannot support hope, because hope requires confidence that the future is anchored to something more stable than desire or chance.

When these failures occur, they are often treated as personal shortcomings. People are told to manage expectations, adjust outlooks, or reinterpret the problem. Rarely do we ask whether the ground itself is capable of holding what we ask it to bear.

Sand can absorb effort, but it cannot anchor life. It shifts under pressure. It intrudes into everything. It obscures vision when disturbed. And it resists growth, because nothing can take root where the surface is always moving.

These are not moral accusations.

They are structural realities.

Why Instability Feels Like a Problem

At this point, it is fair to ask: isn't instability simply part of being human?

If it were, we would accept it more easily. But we do not. We experience instability as a problem, not merely an inconvenience. We expect justice to matter. We assume that truth should not change with circumstances. We long for permanence even when we deny it.

These expectations are not learned preferences. They are recognitions.

The fact that shifting ground feels wrong is itself evidence that stability is not an illusion. The discomfort points beyond itself. It suggests that the problem is not life, but the foundation on which life is being lived.

The Question Beneath the Questions

This chapter has not asked what you believe.

It has asked what you rely on.

Not whether your explanations are sincere, but whether they can bear weight. Not whether they help you cope, but whether they can sustain meaning, justice, and hope over time.

The question beneath all the others is simple, but not easy:

Where can anyone actually stand?

That question does not yet have an answer here. But it is the right question. And until it is faced honestly, no amount of effort or adjustment will make the ground beneath us settle.

Summary

This chapter has examined the instability many experience in modern life and suggested that the problem may not be internal weakness, but unreliable ground. Explanations that shift under pressure require constant effort, erode moral clarity, and fail to sustain justice, guilt, or hope.

Sand can absorb activity for a time, but it cannot serve as a foundation. When life is lived on shifting ground, nothing fully rests, and growth becomes difficult.

The unease many feel is not a personal failure.

It is a signal—pointing toward a deeper question about whether solid ground exists at all.

That question will guide what follows.

Application: Questions of Ground

1. What explanations do you currently rely on to give your life meaning or stability?

2. When those explanations are tested by failure, injustice, or guilt, do they hold—or do they shift?

3. Which areas of your life require the most effort simply to stay balanced?

4. Where do you sense instability most clearly: identity, morality, purpose, or hope?

5. Do you experience instability as merely uncomfortable—or as something that feels fundamentally wrong? Why?

6. What would it mean for life to rest on ground that does not move?

Where to Stand

2

Why We Keep Standing on the Sand

The Question We Avoid

If unstable ground were merely an accident, the solution would be simple: step off it. Find something firmer. Adjust course. But that is not what usually happens. Even when explanations fail, even when instability becomes exhausting, people often remain committed to the same ground.

This raises an uncomfortable question—one we tend to avoid.

If the ground beneath us cannot hold, why do we keep standing on it?

It is tempting to answer with sympathy alone. We point to upbringing, culture, trauma, or lack of options.

These factors matter, and they should not be dismissed. But they do not tell the whole story. People are not merely placed on unstable ground; they often choose it—and defend that choice even when it costs them.

One reason for this is simple and unsettling: sand, for all its exhaustion, is **compliant**.

Shifting ground may be tiring, but it is negotiable. Sand moves when we push it. It can be reshaped, re-leveled, reinterpreted. When something goes wrong, the surface can be smoothed over. Failure can be reframed. Guilt can be softened into growth. A collapse can be renamed a "journey."

On sand, meaning is adjustable. Standards can be lowered without being openly denied. Consequences can be explained rather than faced. The ground may not be solid, but it yields to us. That yielding feels merciful—even when it is quietly corrosive.

Rock is different.

Rock does not shift to accommodate us. It does not move when we fall. It does not rearrange itself to make our missteps feel less severe. On solid ground, failure is not negotiable. It must be reckoned with rather than reinterpreted. Truth does not flex to preserve our self-understanding.

This is why, for many, the inflexibility of truth feels harsher than the fatigue of instability. We choose the exhaustion of sand over the unyielding nature of what is solid. We prefer ground that will adjust to us, even if it never truly holds us.

Closely related to this preference is the illusion of control.

Life on unstable ground requires constant management—monitoring language, adjusting explanations, recalibrating identity. While this is draining, it provides a powerful psychological reward: **the feeling of agency**. As long as we are managing the instability, we feel involved. We are doing something. We are steering.

This is why many would rather be the captain of a sinking ship than a subject on a stable continent.

A sinking ship allows command, decision, motion. A solid continent demands submission to what already is. One preserves the sense of authority; the other requires relinquishing it.

The illusion is subtle but persuasive. Managing instability feels like leadership, even when the direction is wrong. Struggle feels like purpose. Motion feels like control. The fact that the ship is taking on water becomes secondary to the satisfaction of holding the wheel.

It is like a person in a small rowboat, drifting toward a waterfall. An anchor lies within reach, but dropping it would mean admitting that steering alone is not enough. *"I can fix this!"* So the person keeps rowing, adjusting course, correcting drift—enjoying the sensation of control—while the current continues its quiet, relentless pull.

The problem is not ignorance. It is preference.

For many, there is also a deeper reason: the sand is familiar.

The sinking feeling, the constant adjustment, the low-grade anxiety—these are not merely endured; they are home. For those who have spent their lives balancing on unstable ground, instability feels normal. Vigilance feels responsible. Rest feels dangerous.

The idea of firm ground can feel disorienting.

Someone who has lived on a tightrope learns to associate balance with tension. The muscles are always engaged. The eyes are always scanning. When that person finally steps onto flat, unmoving ground, the absence of motion can produce vertigo. The stillness feels unsafe—not because it is, but because it is unfamiliar.

This is why some resist stability even when they long for it. The Rock feels "dangerously" different. It removes the need for constant adjustment, but in doing so, it removes familiar coping strategies. It exposes how much of life has been organized around staying upright rather than standing secure.

We do not only stay on sand because we like it. We stay because the alternative feels like stepping into a foreign land without a map.

There is also a social reason—one that rarely gets named.

Everyone else is on the sandbar.

Shifting ground is crowded ground. The rules are shared. The language is familiar. The risks are distributed. When everyone is balancing, no one stands out. When everyone is adjusting, instability feels normal—even virtuous.

Stepping onto solid ground often means stepping away from the crowd. It can look like rigidity. It can sound like judgment. It can feel like betrayal. The person who steps onto the Rock is no longer participating in the collective negotiation of meaning, and that withdrawal is noticed.

Middle school dynamics never truly disappear; they scale. Belonging is still regulated. Deviance is still penalized. Safety is still found in numbers.

So we remain on the sand not only because it shifts, but because it is populated. The social cost of the

Rock often feels higher than the personal cost of sinking—at least in the short term.

This is why unstable ground is defended so fiercely.

To admit that the ground cannot hold would require more than adjustment. It would require surrender. It would mean acknowledging that some things are not ours to redefine—that truth, responsibility, and judgment may exist independently of our preferences.

That admission feels risky. It threatens control. It disrupts belonging. And it raises a question we may not feel ready to answer:

What if the problem is not that we have failed to manage the ground—but that the ground was never ours to manage at all?

Control Feels Safer Than Trust

One reason unstable ground continues to attract loyalty is not power, but familiarity.

For many, the feeling of standing on sand—adjusting, compensating, bracing—has become so normal that anything else feels wrong. Instability is not experienced as danger so much as atmosphere. It is the air people have learned to breathe.

Those who have spent their lives balancing rarely remember what it is like to stand on something that does not move.

This is why firm ground can feel threatening. Stability requires a different kind of posture. On shifting ground, balance is active and tense; the body is always compensating. On solid ground, balance is passive. Weight is received rather than managed. Nothing needs to be corrected.

For someone who has lived on a tightrope, this change can produce vertigo.

A tightrope walker trusts tension. Muscles are engaged. Eyes are fixed. The danger is visible and immediate. But when that same person steps onto a wide, unmoving floor, the absence of motion can feel disorienting. The body searches for instability that is no longer there. The stillness feels unsafe—not because it is, but because it is unfamiliar.

This is how the Rock can feel to someone who has only known sand.

Stability does not register as relief at first. It registers as loss of orientation. The ground does not respond. It does not adjust. It does not explain itself. It simply holds—and that very fact can feel dangerous to those who have learned to survive by constant adjustment.

So people remain on the sand not only because they want control, but because the Rock feels alien. It demands a way of standing they have never practiced.

There is also a quieter, more tragic calculation at work.

People often perform an unspoken cost–benefit analysis, and the sand usually wins.

The sand is miserable, but it is predictable. It sinks, but at a rate that feels familiar. The anxiety is constant, but it is known. The effort is exhausting, but it has a rhythm. People learn how much they can tolerate, how far they can lean, how often they must correct themselves to stay upright.

The Rock, by contrast, represents an unknown.

It promises stability, but not on terms we control. It offers rest, but not familiarity. It requires trust rather than technique. And trust, for someone shaped by instability, feels far riskier than managed misery.

This is why people often choose miserable certainty over uncertain hope.

The sand is failing, but it is failing in ways we recognize. We understand its disappointments. We know where it gives way. The Rock might hold—but stepping onto it would mean relinquishing the only system we know how to navigate.

So we stay where the suffering is calculated rather than unknown.

This is not cowardice. It is human tragedy. People do not cling to instability because they love it, but because they fear what they cannot yet imagine.

There is still another weight holding people in place: the weight of others.

The sand is where the crowd stands.

As Chapter 1 showed, modern life is already structured like an endless middle school—status-conscious, reactive, watchful. The sandbar is populated. Everyone is balancing together. Everyone is negotiating meaning together. No one is alone there.

Stepping onto solid ground is not merely a change of foundation; it is a change of location—and therefore a change of community.

The one who steps off the sand no longer participates in the collective recalibration of reality. They stop adjusting their footing in sync with everyone else. They stop explaining instability as normal. And that departure is noticed.

Standing on the Rock can look like withdrawal. It can sound like refusal. It can feel like abandonment to those who remain behind.

So the choice is rarely framed honestly. It is not stability versus instability. It is belonging versus standing alone.

For many, the social cost of the Rock feels heavier than the personal cost of sinking—at least for now.

And so the sand continues to feel safer than trust.

When Responsibility Becomes a Burden

Unstable ground also offers a way to manage responsibility—but only at first glance.

When standards are fixed, responsibility is unavoidable. Actions have consequences that cannot be negotiated away. Guilt must be faced rather than reinterpreted. Justice must be reckoned with rather than deferred. Solid ground does not argue back. It simply stands.

Sand, by contrast, allows responsibility to be softened.

When meaning is flexible, responsibility becomes negotiable. When standards shift, guilt can be reframed as misunderstanding, conditioning, or misalignment. When outcomes are explained primarily by circumstance, agency dissolves into complexity. What matters most is no longer what happened, but how the story is told.

This does not eliminate responsibility—it relocates it. Responsibility is shifted from moral reality to personal narrative.

And that shift comes at a cost.

On shifting ground, a person must become a full-time lawyer for the self.

Without a fixed standard to appeal to, every situation requires interpretation. Motives must be clarified. Context must be supplied. Explanations must be curated carefully to ensure that one remains intelligible—and innocent—within the story being told. One must always appear as either the protagonist or the victim, but never the culprit.

This work never ends.

Each new event requires a new brief. Each accusation—internal or external—demands rebuttal. Each failure must be reclassified so it does not threaten the story's coherence. The self becomes both client and counsel, constantly defending its own account of reality.

This is not freedom. It is exhaustion.

Negotiable responsibility feels lighter only because the weight is being carried indirectly. Instead of answering to something solid, the person must maintain an interpretation of themselves that can survive scrutiny. The labor is quieter, but it is relentless.

Over time, something else begins to erode.

When responsibility is consistently softened into circumstance, agency fades with it. If nothing is truly my fault because of systems, pressures, or histories, then nothing is truly my achievement either. If my failures are never finally mine, my successes cannot be either.

The same move that protects us from guilt quietly strips us of dignity.

A self who cannot be held accountable cannot be honored. A person who is never responsible is never truly powerful. By dissolving responsibility into complexity, we do not merely avoid blame—we weaken our own sense of worth.

This is one of the great ironies of life on sand. We choose it to hide our sins, but we end up losing ourselves in the process. Identity becomes thin, defensive, and provisional. The self survives, but it no longer stands.

The ground beneath it is too soft.

The difference between fixed standards and shifting ones can be felt more than argued.

A fixed standard is like a stone wall. It does not move. If you run into it, the impact hurts—but you know where you are. The boundary is clear. The resistance is real. You can orient yourself by it, even when it confronts you.

Shifting standards are not like a wall. They are like fog or marshland.

You do not collide with them. You drift into them. There is no moment of impact, no clear resistance— only gradual sinking. Nothing pushes back hard enough to stop you, but nothing supports you either. You lose traction without realizing it. Direction becomes uncertain. Movement becomes effortful, then futile.

This is the danger of sand.

Its threat is not collision, but collapse. Not judgment, but erosion. Not confrontation, but the slow loss of friction that makes standing possible at all.

Responsibility softened enough to avoid guilt is responsibility softened enough to erase the self.

And so what begins as relief becomes burden. What feels like mercy becomes maintenance. What promises freedom becomes a life spent defending one's own interpretation of events—on ground that cannot hold still long enough to justify anyone.

Burying and Unburying

Sand has a peculiar quality: it hides things easily, but it does not keep them hidden.

This is part of what makes unstable ground so attractive. It offers concealment without confrontation. It allows us to believe that what is unseen is resolved. If no one is watching, if no record remains, if the surface looks undisturbed, then the problem feels contained.

But sand shifts.

One of the earliest biblical images of this illusion is found in the life of Moses—long before law, covenant, or calling define him.

Moses saw an Egyptian beating a Hebrew. He intervened violently. Then the text pauses on a telling detail: he looked this way and that way, and when he saw that there was no man, he slew the Egyptian and hid him in the sand.

That moment captures the logic of life on sand perfectly.

Moses did not deny the act. He did not justify it. He buried it. He scanned the horizon, confirmed the absence of witnesses, and trusted the ground beneath him to cooperate. The solution was situational: the right place, the right timing, the right concealment.

As long as no one was watching, the problem felt managed.

But the issue was never the witnesses.

It was the ground.

The sand did what sand always does. It shifted. The hidden act surfaced. The word spread. And the very thing Moses thought he had buried became the event that drove him into exile. His secret did not merely fail to stay hidden—it reshaped his entire future.

The irony is sharp. Moses' attempt to manage guilt situationally did not preserve his life; it fractured it. The sand did not protect him. It betrayed him—not because it was malicious, but because it could not hold.

This is not an ancient failure. It is a familiar pattern.

We think we are safe as long as no one is watching. We assume that silence equals resolution. We choose quiet places—relationally, morally, emotionally—to bury what would complicate our story. We forget that the ground we are standing on is already moving.

What is buried in sand is never finished with us.

The Old Testament sacrificial system confronts this same reality from a different angle.

It is often misunderstood as primitive ritual or religious performance, but at its core it functioned as moral acknowledgment. It refused to let guilt be buried. It forced weight into the open.

In a world where the instinct is to hide wrongdoing, the sacrificial system did something counterintuitive: it externalized guilt. Wrong was not explained away or absorbed quietly into personal narrative. It was placed —visibly, deliberately—on something else.

An animal bore the weight. Blood was shed. Cost was incurred.

This did not remove guilt permanently. The Scriptures themselves insist that the blood of bulls and goats could not change the ground beneath human reality. But the sacrifices served another purpose: they prevented denial. They made delay visible. They ensured that moral weight could not be quietly buried and forgotten.

The system acknowledged what life on sand tries to avoid—that guilt is not resolved by time or concealment. It must be dealt with, even if only provisionally.

The sacrifices were not the solution. They were a restraint. They held the pressure in place until something could bear it fully.

This brings us back to the deeper problem.

Reality presses upward.

Guilt, like all truth, has a kind of buoyancy. It behaves less like dirt and more like air or water. The harder it is pushed down, the more forcefully it tries to rise. Anyone who has tried to hold a ball underwater knows the sensation. At first it seems manageable. But the deeper it is submerged, the more effort is required. Muscles strain. Attention narrows. Fatigue sets in.

Eventually, something gives.

This is why buried guilt returns—not because people are weak, but because reality resists suppression. What is hidden requires energy to keep hidden. What is unacknowledged must be continually restrained.

This effort is one source of the quiet exhaustion that marks modern life.

We are not only tired from living. We are tired from holding things down.

From managing stories. From maintaining explanations. From ensuring that what lies beneath the surface does not break through at the wrong moment. The ground beneath us is unstable, and so the work of concealment never ends.

Sand does not absorb moral weight. It delays it.

And delay, over time, becomes heavier than exposure.

What Moses learned in the wilderness, and what the sacrificial system kept before Israel's eyes, is what we are slow to accept: there is no quiet enough place to bury what reality insists on bringing to the surface.

The question is not whether buried things will return.

It is how much effort will be spent trying to keep them down—and how long the ground will pretend to cooperate.

One reason adjustment never ends is that language itself has lost its footing. Words were once bridges— shared tools that allowed people to meet across difference. Increasingly, they have become traps. Terms are not merely redefined; they are de-defined. We are told that words mean only what the speaker intends, and that misunderstanding is therefore a moral failure of the listener. But language that carries no shared meaning cannot carry responsibility either. Rather than producing inclusion, this collapse produces isolation. Communication becomes impossible not because people refuse to speak, but because there is no longer common ground on which words can land.

Language that floats cannot confront, correct, or reconcile—it can only be managed.

Autonomy Without Foundation

At the center of this pattern lies a deeper issue: autonomy without foundation.

To live autonomously is not simply to make choices. It is to claim authority over the meaning of those choices. It is to stand as judge not only of actions, but of the standards by which they are evaluated.

At first, this feels like freedom.

But over time, autonomy closes in on itself.

When there is no external standard, judgment becomes circular. The self becomes both defendant and judge, both witness and jury. There is no higher court to appeal to, no final authority beyond one's own evaluation.

This creates what might be called the internal courtroom.

Every action is reviewed. Every motive is examined. Every failure is argued over. The case never adjourns.

There is no moment when judgment is finished, because the one issuing the verdict is the same one who must live with it.

Autonomy does not remove judgment; it internalizes it.

And internalized judgment is relentless.

There is no pardon that feels final, because the one granting it knows the weaknesses of the one receiving it. The judge is always present, always observing, always aware of unspoken motives and half-hidden compromises. Acquittal feels provisional. Approval must be renewed.

This is why so many people feel they are "doing everything right" and yet feel no rest. The problem is not effort. It is that there is no authority capable of declaring the case closed.

Autonomy promises liberation from judgment, but it often results in its intensification. The judge is always watching—and never fully satisfied.

Over time, this posture produces fragility.

A standard you create is a standard you can also break.

If I decide what "good" means, then my goodness is only as stable as my mood, my consistency, or my latest success. If my worth depends on my own evaluation, then it must be continually defended—against failure, against criticism, against time itself.

This is why certainty so often gives way to defensiveness.

When someone questions a self-generated standard, they are not merely disagreeing with an idea. They are threatening the foundation itself. Debate feels personal because it is personal. Critique feels hostile because there is nothing beneath the standard to absorb the pressure.

Identity built on self-evaluation cannot relax. It must protect itself constantly, because it has nowhere else to stand.

This defensiveness is often misread as arrogance or pride. More often, it is fear. A foundation made of one's own opinions must be guarded carefully, because if it cracks, everything above it collapses.

Yet it is important to understand why many people adopted autonomy in the first place.

For a great number, autonomy was not rebellion—it was survival.

Trust was abused. Institutions failed. Churches wounded rather than healed. Families fractured. Authorities promised protection and delivered harm.

In such conditions, reliance on external standards felt dangerous.

So people turned inward.

Autonomy became a fortress. If no one else could be trusted, at least the self could be defended. If no external authority could be relied upon, at least personal judgment could provide safety.

This move made sense. It was often necessary.

But a fortress built on sand is still sinking ground.

Autonomy can shield for a time, but without foundation it cannot sustain. The walls grow higher. The vigilance increases. The exhaustion deepens. What once felt like protection slowly becomes imprisonment.

The tragedy is not that people chose autonomy. It is that a strategy meant to preserve dignity has begun to erode it. The self was never meant to carry the full weight of judgment, meaning, and justification alone.

Autonomy without foundation does not collapse all at once.

It tightens.

And the tighter it becomes, the more fragile it feels.

Why We Defend Unstable Ground

If unstable ground produces exhaustion, guilt, and fragility, a reasonable question remains: why is it defended so fiercely?

The answer is not ignorance. It is **investment**.

By the time many people begin to sense that the ground beneath them cannot hold, they have already built a life upon it. Years—sometimes decades—have been spent constructing identity, reputation, relationships, and meaning on that foundation. Choices have been justified. Sacrifices have been made. Personas have been shaped carefully to survive and succeed in a shifting environment.

To admit that the ground is unstable at that point feels catastrophic.

It would not mean adjusting a belief or refining a philosophy. It would mean questioning whether the entire structure was built in the wrong place. It would feel like confessing that one's life's work rests on something that was never solid.

This is why the sand must be defended.

The more that has been built on it, the more fiercely it must be described as stone. The greater the investment, the higher the emotional cost of admitting error. What is at stake is not merely truth, but dignity. Not merely explanation, but meaning.

People do not defend unstable ground because they love it. They defend it because abandoning it feels like **self-erasure**.

There is also another fear—quieter, but just as powerful.

The fear of the in-between.

Stepping off unstable ground is not experienced as an immediate transfer. It feels like a gap. A moment where the foot leaves what is known before it has landed on something else. That space—however brief—feels terrifying.

For many, autonomy has been the only ground they have ever trusted. Outside of it, they imagine nothingness. Chaos. Dependence. Loss of self. The thought of relinquishing control feels less like humility and more like annihilation.

So people stay.

Not because they believe the sand will hold, but because a sinking foundation feels preferable to no foundation at all. Even instability offers something to stand on—however briefly. Even collapse feels safer than surrender to the unknown.

This fear is rarely articulated. Instead, it is disguised as caution, skepticism, or maturity. But beneath those labels lies a simple impulse: better the ground that is failing than the ground I cannot yet see.

This helps explain another common response— **criticism**.

When confronted with the possibility of solid ground, many do not engage it honestly. They attack it.

Alternatives are dismissed as simplistic, dangerous, outdated, or naïve. Faith is caricatured. External truth is reduced to power plays or psychological crutches. The Rock is treated as though it must be no more stable than the sand.

This criticism is often assumed to be intellectual. Frequently, it is defensive.

The existence of solid ground is unsettling to those sinking slowly. It suggests that instability is not inevitable. That collapse is not merely the human condition. That something firmer may have been available all along.

And that suggestion carries an unspoken accusation —not moral, but existential: *What if this did not have to be this hard?*

Rather than face that question, it is easier to level the field. To insist that everything shifts. To claim that all foundations are equally unstable. If everything is sand, then no one has made a mistake. No one is sinking more than anyone else. Shame is neutralized by universality.

So we whistle past the graveyard of our own instability.

We critique the Rock not because it lacks weight, but because its presence exposes what we have trusted. If the Rock stands, then the sand has been a poor substitute. And admitting that would require more than intellectual honesty—it would require letting go.

This is why unstable ground is not merely endured. It is protected.

Because to stop defending it would mean facing the possibility that stability was never impossible—only costly.

And that is a question many are not yet ready to answer.

The Responsibility Beneath the Instability

This chapter does not argue that people are intentionally choosing chaos. It argues something more restrained—and more demanding: that we often prefer unstable ground we can manage to solid ground we cannot control.

Where to Stand

That preference carries responsibility.

In modern culture, responsibility is often treated as an accusation. Victimhood, by contrast, has become a form of social currency. To be wronged is to be validated. To be harmed is to be explained. These recognitions matter. Real harm should never be dismissed.

But victimhood, by itself, offers no way out.

A victim is acted upon. A victim waits. A victim may be justified—but is rarely free. When instability is explained entirely by external forces, dignity quietly erodes. The self becomes weightless, carried wherever the ground shifts.

Responsibility restores weight.

To acknowledge responsibility is not to deny harm or excuse injustice. It is to reclaim agency. A responsible person is not a leaf in the wind, but someone with feet. Even if those feet are currently standing on sand, they are still feet.

This matters.

If instability were purely imposed, no change would be possible. But if we acknowledge—even quietly—that we chose the ground we are standing on, then movement becomes conceivable. Responsibility does not condemn. It hands back the keys.

Responsibility is not a sentence. It is access.

This helps explain why people often remain in instability long after it has proven itself unreliable.

We become experts in manageable chaos.

A failing relationship is painful, but familiar. A broken tool frustrates, but we know its quirks. We learn how much pressure it can take, where it slips, how to compensate for its weaknesses. Over time, we stop asking whether it works and focus instead on how to keep it limping along.

We know how this fails.

This familiarity becomes strangely comforting. The dysfunction has a pattern. The disappointment has a rhythm. We have learned how to sink slowly.

Stepping away would require learning something new —risking a different kind of failure. So we stay, not because we love what is broken, but because we have mastered its limitations.

The same logic governs life on sand.

We are not choosing instability because we enjoy it. We are choosing it because we know how to manage it. We have developed skills for survival—explanation, adjustment, reinterpretation—that make collapse feel gradual rather than sudden.

But slow sinking is still sinking.

This is where responsibility changes everything.

If the problem were "the world," our default response would make sense. We would blame systems, cultures, structures, and generations before us. And fixing the world would appear not only logical, but noble. Every age has been drawn to that solution. Each has believed that with the right reforms, the right leaders, the right awareness, or the right revolution, instability could finally be resolved. Yet history tells a sobering story. Attempts to repair the world at the level of systems alone have not produced stability; they have multiplied complexity, shifted power, and often deepened the very fractures they sought to heal. The promise is always the same: change everything, and things will finally hold. The result is always disappointment. The solution is not only unrealistic; it is paralyzing. It places responsibility at a scale no individual can bear and leaves people waiting for forces beyond their reach—while life continues to sink beneath their feet.

But if the problem is foundation—if the issue is where one stands—then the scope of the problem narrows dramatically.

It becomes personal, but not crushing. Specific, but not overwhelming. The question shifts from Why is everything unstable? to Where am I standing?

And that question can be answered.

This is the quiet good news of this chapter.

Responsibility does not trap us inside ourselves. It opens the door to movement. It makes change imaginable. It turns instability from an unalterable condition into a diagnosable location.

The ground beneath us may still be sand.

But if we can name that truth honestly—without excuse and without despair—then for the first time, stepping off it becomes possible.

Not because we are strong enough.

But because we are no longer pretending the ground can hold.

The Question Deepens

Chapter 1 asked whether the ground beneath us can hold.

This chapter has asked why we remain on ground that cannot.

Together, these questions rule out simple fixes.

By the time most people recognize instability, they have already tried to correct it. New strategies are adopted. Better habits are formed. Perspectives are refined. Language is adjusted. The hope is always the same: this change will finally make things settle.

But the cycle keeps repeating.

This is the exhaustion of adjustment.

When the floor is moving, no amount of rearranging helps. A better chair does not stabilize a shifting foundation. A more comfortable routine does not stop the ground from giving way beneath it. Even sincere effort only improves the experience of instability—it does not remove it.

This is why so many feel tired without knowing why. They are not failing to live well. They are trying to stabilize something that cannot be stabilized from within.

The problem is not the furniture of life.

It is the foundation.

This also clarifies a crucial distinction.

Most books offer information. They explain the problem, refine awareness, and provide insight. Information has value—but information alone cannot relocate a person. Knowing that sand is sinking does not stop the sinking. You can analyze it, map it, even master its properties—and still drown.

You can earn a doctorate in sand and never find solid ground.

What is being suggested here is not an intellectual ascent, but a transfer. Not a change of opinion, but a change of location. If stability exists, it cannot be achieved by understanding alone. It must be entered. Weight must be moved. Standing must occur somewhere else.

This matters because it reframes what comes next.

The chapters that follow will not simply be interesting. They will be demanding. Not emotionally manipulative, but existentially serious. They will not ask merely whether an idea is compelling, but whether a person is willing to stand somewhere different.

At this point, the question is no longer abstract.

Once instability is seen for what it is, staying becomes a different kind of burden. You can no longer pretend the ground is solid. You can no longer explain exhaustion as immaturity or restlessness as weakness. What was once tolerable becomes heavy with awareness.

This is not pressure imposed from outside. It is clarity pressing from within.

The possibility that solid ground exists changes everything. It makes continued adjustment feel less like wisdom and more like delay. It introduces a quiet unrest—not panic, but tension. Not fear, but inevitability.

The question has deepened.

It is no longer Is this ground unstable?

It is Where can anyone actually stand?

That question does not yet have an answer here.

But now it cannot be ignored.

And until it is faced honestly, no amount of strategy, insight, or effort will make the ground beneath us settle.

Summary

This chapter has examined why people often remain on unstable ground even after its failure becomes clear. The problem is not ignorance or lack of effort. It is preference, familiarity, investment, and fear.

Sand is exhausting, but it is negotiable. It yields to interpretation, allows responsibility to be softened, and permits guilt to be buried—at least temporarily. Over time, this produces a life of constant adjustment: managing narratives, defending identity, and maintaining a sense of control that never quite delivers rest. Autonomy promises freedom, but without foundation it intensifies judgment, erodes dignity, and closes the self into an exhausting internal courtroom.

Instability persists not only because of external pressures, but because it feels safer than surrendering to ground that does not move. Many have invested years building a life on sand; admitting its instability feels like admitting personal loss. Others fear the unknown space between leaving familiar ground and standing somewhere new. Still others defend the sand by leveling every alternative, insisting that all ground must shift—so no one need face the shame of sinking.

Yet beneath these defenses lies a deeper truth: responsibility remains. Not as accusation, but as agency. To acknowledge that we chose where we stand is not to deny harm or excuse injustice; it is to reclaim the dignity of movement. If instability were only "the world's" fault, no change would be conceivable. But if the problem is foundation, then the question narrows to a size that can be faced.

This chapter has ruled out simple fixes. Better strategies, clearer insight, or greater effort cannot stabilize shifting ground. Information alone cannot relocate a person. Knowing the sand is sinking does not stop the sinking.

What remains is a deeper question—one that cannot be resolved by adjustment or explanation:

Where can anyone actually stand?

That question does not yet have an answer here. But it now carries weight. And until it is answered, no amount of management will make the ground beneath us hold.

Application: Questions of Ground

1. Where do you experience the greatest desire to remain in control—meaning, morality, or identity?

2. How do you typically respond when guilt or responsibility surfaces: confrontation, reinterpretation, or concealment?

3. What explanations allow you the most flexibility— and what do they cost you over time?

4. In what ways does autonomy feel safer than trust?

5. What might you lose by standing on ground that does not move?

6. What might you gain?

Where to Stand

3

When Justice Has Nowhere to Stand

The Demand We Cannot Silence

There is one human response that refuses to disappear, no matter how thoroughly it is explained away: outrage.

It does not need to be taught. It does not wait for permission. It arrives uninvited and fully formed. Something is wrong. Someone has crossed a line. This should not be happening.

In an age that prides itself on nuance, outrage remains blunt.

Modern digital culture has only amplified this reality. Social media functions as a global megaphone, broadcasting moral reaction at unprecedented speed and scale. Every day brings new judgments, new condemnations, new demands for accountability. Even in a secular and pluralistic society, the need for justice has not diminished. If anything, it has intensified.

What has disappeared is not the demand—but the place to put it.

We have not lost the idea of a judge.

We have lost a seat for one to sit on.

This creates a profound tension. Many insist that morality is constructed, contextual, and contingent. Truth is said to be fluid. Standards are declared negotiable. Yet the moment an injustice is encountered, this careful language evaporates.

Consider a simple, hypothetical scenario.

Imagine that someone manipulates your reputation— knowingly, maliciously, and publicly. They distort your words, damage your standing, and cost you something real: a job, a relationship, an opportunity you worked years to build. You confront them, and they shrug. They explain that perspectives differ, that truth is subjective, that harm is a matter of interpretation.

In that moment, something ignites.

The language of nuance collapses. You do not respond with theory. You do not appeal to complexity. You say, That is wrong. Not unfortunate. Not complicated. Wrong.

Even the most committed relativist becomes certain when injustice is personal. The instinct is immediate and absolute. There is no hesitation, no seminar-length qualification. Justice feels less like an opinion and more like something reality itself demands.

This is the irony at the heart of modern moral life.

Those who insist that morality is a social construct often become the most uncompromising when they are wronged. They may deny the existence of objective justice in theory, but they appeal to it instinctively. The demand surfaces before reflection can suppress it.

Which raises an unavoidable question:

If justice is not real, why does it feel so non-negotiable?

This demand cannot be silenced. It can be redirected, rationalized, or delayed—but it always returns. And when there is no shared foundation on which to stand, it turns inward.

This brings us back to the internal courtroom.

In Chapter 2, we saw how autonomy without foundation traps the self in endless self-evaluation. Here, the problem intensifies. The demand for justice continues to press, but there is no solid ground to resolve it. No final verdict can be rendered. No authoritative judgment can be trusted.

The courtroom never adjourns.

Every injustice—suffered or committed—must be processed internally. Every grievance must be weighed personally. Every wrong must be judged without appeal. The self becomes responsible not only for meaning, but for justice itself.

This is an unbearable weight.

Outrage without resolution produces exhaustion. Condemnation without conclusion produces cynicism. The demand for justice continues to rise, but without foundation it has nowhere to land. So it circulates— online, relationally, internally—intensifying without ever satisfying.

This is one source of the quiet exhaustion that now marks so many lives.

People are not tired because they no longer care about justice. They are tired because they care deeply—and have no place to put the weight of that care. The demand cannot be silenced, but neither can it be resolved on shifting ground.

Justice insists on something solid.

And until such ground is found, the demand will only grow louder—inside us and all around us.

Justice Without Judgment

When justice is demanded but judgment is refused, the result is a verdict without a court.

The language of justice remains—harm is acknowledged, pain is affirmed, stories are validated —but the mechanism that could actually resolve the wrong is absent. Something has been named as unjust, yet no authoritative judgment is rendered. No responsibility is fixed. No reckoning is completed.

This produces a unique kind of frustration.

Imagine a courtroom where the judge listens carefully to the victim, affirms their suffering, and validates the depth of their pain—but refuses to address the perpetrator. No verdict is issued. No guilt is assigned. No consequences follow. The hearing ends with empathy, but without resolution.

The victim leaves heard, but not vindicated.

The perpetrator leaves unchanged.

And the moral air remains thick with tension.

Nothing has settled.

This is what justice without judgment feels like. It recognizes harm, but it cannot complete the work justice exists to do. The wrong is acknowledged, but it is not answered. And unanswered wrong does not dissipate—it lingers.

On unstable ground, justice inevitably becomes performative.

Without a foundation capable of bearing moral weight, societies resort to symbols. Public apologies are issued. Statements are crafted carefully. Hashtags trend. Rituals of acknowledgment multiply. These actions are not meaningless; they often arise from genuine concern. But they are attempts to restore balance without the gravity required to do so.

They signal belonging. They express solidarity. They perform moral alignment.

What they cannot do is settle accounts.

Because nothing truly rests on sand, justice expressed there must be continually reenacted. Each new outrage requires a new statement. Each unresolved wrong demands fresh performance. The cycle accelerates, not because people are becoming more immoral, but because the ground beneath justice cannot hold its conclusions.

This is why modern justice feels loud but weightless. It moves quickly, but it does not arrive. It reassures momentarily, but it does not resolve. The performance must continue because the problem remains suspended.

Often, this softening of judgment is motivated by compassion.

We learn the stories behind the harm. We trace trauma, environment, and pressure. We understand that people are shaped by forces beyond their control. These insights matter. They deepen understanding and restrain cruelty.

But compassion was never meant to replace judgment—only to inform it.

When compassion is used as a substitute for judgment, justice loses its footing. Accountability is quietly reframed as insensitivity. Responsibility is softened into inevitability. Harm is explained so thoroughly that it is no longer answered.

This creates what might be called justice-free compassion.

In this posture, the suffering of the perpetrator eclipses the suffering they caused. The explanation becomes the exoneration. The moral claim of the victim is acknowledged emotionally, but denied structurally. The message, however unintended, is clear: what happened mattered—but not enough to require an answer.

True justice does not deny complexity. It does not ignore wounds or histories. Compassionate justice can acknowledge struggle while still naming wrong. It can recognize context without dissolving responsibility.

Justice-free compassion cannot.

By removing judgment entirely, it removes the very mechanism that could give compassion meaning. Mercy without truth is not mercy—it is abandonment dressed in kindness.

And so the weight remains.

Sand cannot absorb guilt. It can only cover it, scatter it, or shift it elsewhere. Modern culture speaks often of "moving on" or "letting go," but when moral weight has not been placed on something solid, it does not disappear. It hovers.

Unresolved guilt creates a culture of permanent tension. Resentment simmers beneath civility. Outrage waits for the next trigger. Forgiveness feels impossible, not because people are unwilling, but because nothing has been settled enough to forgive.

Justice without judgment does not heal.

It suspends.

And suspended weight does not rest—it exhausts.

The Weight Justice Carries

Justice is not light.

This is why attempts to make it weightless always fail. They may accelerate moral reaction, amplify outrage, or multiply expressions of concern—but they cannot resolve the demand justice places on reality.

Modern outrage is a case study in this failure.

We live in what might be called a cycle of unmoored fury. A story breaks. A wrong is exposed. Collective anger ignites. For a brief moment—sometimes only hours—there is a powerful sense of moral clarity. We feel aligned. We feel certain. We feel, finally, as though we are standing on solid ground.

And then the ground shifts.

By the next morning, the outrage has splintered. Counter-narratives emerge. New details surface. Attention moves on. A different injustice replaces the last. The fury dissipates—not because justice has been done, but because the weight has nowhere to rest.

The cycle repeats.

This is the intensity of a verdict without the stability of a judge. We experience the emotional force of judgment without the structural capacity to sustain it. Outrage becomes a way to signal belonging—to prove that we stand on the "right side"—but it cannot carry justice forward. It burns hot and fast, then leaves nothing settled behind it.

This unsatisfying quality is not accidental. It reveals a deeper problem.

Justice grounded in negotiated values works only as long as nothing presses too hard against the agreement. Consensus can regulate behavior. It can set norms. It can maintain order—until injustice demands more than alignment.

What happens when consensus shifts?

If justice is merely a social currency, then vindication is temporary. Yesterday's victim may become tomorrow's liability. Today's moral clarity may be recast as tomorrow's embarrassment. No wrong is ever finally answered—only repositioned within a changing landscape of approval.

This creates a world where no one is truly vindicated. People are not declared right or wrong; they are merely aligned or misaligned with the current moral mood. Justice becomes provisional, conditional, and fragile.

And fragility cannot carry weight.

This instability forces responsibility inward.

When there is no final judge, every individual becomes a full-time lawyer for the self. Each action must be defended. Each failure must be contextualized. Each accusation must be answered preemptively, because the jury is always shifting.

The internal courtroom from Chapter 2 expands into public life.

People are exhausted not only by judgment, but by the effort required to avoid it. Innocence must be curated. Explanations must be ready. Silence becomes suspicious. Certainty becomes dangerous. One must constantly monitor how one's story will be received by a court that never adjourns and never settles.

Contrast this with the peace of standing before a Judge who already knows the truth.

Not a judge who must be convinced, but one who sees clearly. Not a jury that fluctuates with opinion, but an authority capable of rendering a verdict that does not require constant defense.

Justice without judgment promises freedom, but delivers permanent trial.

The softening of responsibility intensifies this problem.

On sand, responsibility can always be negotiated away. Failure is reframed as growth. Harm is explained as conditioning. Wrong is diluted into misalignment. These explanations often contain truth —but when they replace moral naming, justice loses its grip.

If everything is context, nothing is culpable.

If every failure is inevitable, no action is accountable.

If wrong is endlessly softened, it is never answered.

This does not produce mercy. It produces moral paralysis.

True justice requires responsibility with weight. It requires the ability to say, without qualification or cruelty, This was wrong. Not unfortunate. Not merely complex. Wrong.

Without that weight, justice becomes theater. Outrage becomes ritual. Compassion becomes evasion. And we find ourselves whistling past the graveyard of our own instability—busy, loud, and morally exhausted.

Justice carries weight because reality demands it.

And sand cannot carry what justice requires.

Why Forgiveness Also Needs Ground

Few words ring more hollow to the deeply wronged than *let it go*.

The advice is usually well-meant. It is offered as a path to peace, a release from bitterness, a way forward. But on unstable ground, it often lands as an additional burden. The one who has been harmed is asked to relinquish something heavy without being told where that weight is supposed to go.

On sand, "letting go" does not remove weight.

It merely drops it.

Serious wrong has moral gravity. It presses downward. It reshapes relationships. It alters trust, memory, and identity. When that gravity is ignored or minimized, it does not disappear. It hovers—over conversations, over silence, over time itself—creating a simmering resentment that sand cannot absorb.

This is why forced forgiveness so often fails. It asks victims to perform a moral feat while standing on ground that is already giving way.

True forgiveness does not deny the weight of what happened. It begins by acknowledging it fully.

Forgiveness is not pretending the harm did not occur. It is not minimizing the offense to preserve peace. It is not reframing evil as misunderstanding or pain as misalignment. Those moves do not forgive; they obscure.

On sand, forgiveness becomes cheap.

Cheap forgiveness keeps relationships functioning by agreement rather than healing. It smooths over conflict, restores surface harmony, and avoids confrontation. But because the underlying weight has never been addressed, it returns—sometimes quietly, sometimes explosively. The relationship survives, but trust does not deepen. The wound closes poorly, because it was never cleaned.

Denial is not mercy. It is postponement.

This is why forgiveness, like justice, requires ground.

Consider the image of a miry pit. If you are sinking— your footing unstable, your strength taxed—and someone tells you to forgive, they are asking you to perform an act of release while you are still struggling to stand. The demand itself becomes cruel, not because forgiveness is wrong, but because the conditions make it impossible.

Forgiveness is not a display of the victim's strength. It is an act made possible by where the weight has already been placed.

Only when the full moral reality of the wrong has been absorbed—named, judged, accounted for—can forgiveness become an act of freedom rather than self-betrayal. Forgiveness does not require the victim to carry the weight forever; it requires that the weight be carried somewhere else.

This is the difference ground makes.

When there is something solid beneath justice— something capable of bearing guilt without cracking— then forgiveness is no longer an act of denial. It becomes an act of trust. Not trust in the offender's reform, and not trust in one's own resilience, but trust that the wrong has been dealt with honestly.

Without that assurance, forgiveness collapses into sentimentality. It sounds noble, but it asks the wounded to pretend that gravity does not exist.

Forgiveness needs a Rock.

Not because victims are weak, but because they were never meant to carry the full weight of moral debt alone. When justice has somewhere to stand—when the offense is neither ignored nor endlessly suspended—then forgiveness becomes possible. Not easy. Not immediate. But real.

Later, we will return to the claim that the resurrection stands as evidence of completion—that guilt and justice are not eternally deferred, but truly answered. For now, it is enough to see the necessity of ground.

Forgiveness does not float.

It does not erase weight.

It releases it—only after it has been carried.

And sand cannot do that work.

Judgment as a Moral Necessity

Judgment is often treated as the enemy of compassion. In practice, the opposite is true.

Judgment says that actions matter. It declares that choices carry weight, that human behavior is not noise or accident, but moral action with real consequence. A world without judgment is not a merciful world—it is a world that quietly treats people as insignificant.

To be judged is to be taken seriously.

Consider the difference between a person whose actions are always explained away and a person who is held responsible. The first is rendered weightless. Their choices are traced endlessly to trauma, conditioning, or circumstance until nothing meaningful remains. They are not condemned—but neither are they trusted. Their actions are no longer theirs in any consequential sense.

The second is treated as a moral agent.

Where to Stand

To be judged is to be recognized as someone whose decisions matter enough to be answered. It affirms that one's life is not merely reactive, but purposeful. That what one does has significance beyond the moment.

If nothing we do is judge-able, then nothing we do truly matters.

Just as a building requires a foundation to stand against the wind, a person requires a standard of judgment to have standing in the world. Without it, identity becomes weightless—subject to drift, pressure, and reinterpretation. We become leaves in the wind rather than people with feet on the ground.

This is why the removal of judgment creates a vacuum rather than peace.

Sand does not eliminate judgment.

It redistributes it.

When judgment no longer rests on something solid—something stable, true, and authoritative—it migrates to other sources. The crowd becomes the court. Visibility becomes evidence. Power becomes verdict.

Modern social shaming is not the absence of judgment; it is judgment without foundation.

In such systems, there is no fixed standard—only fluctuating outrage. Accusation spreads quickly, but resolution never arrives. The punishment is public and indefinite. Apologies may be demanded, but forgiveness is never assured. There is no mechanism for restoration, only erasure or exile.

Because there is no Rock beneath the judgment, it cannot settle. It must be reapplied again and again. What matters is not truth, but influence. Not repentance, but alignment. Not justice, but survival.

This is judgment at its most exhausting and least humane.

True judgment protects the victim precisely because it refuses to dissolve wrong into misfortune.

When wrongdoing is not judged, the victim's outrage is subtly reframed as maladjustment. Their anger is treated as excess emotion rather than a right response to reality. The harm is acknowledged emotionally, but denied morally.

Judgment is the only thing that can look a victim in the eye and say, You are right to be angry. This was wrong.

Without judgment, the victim is left alone in the miry pit—affirmed, perhaps, but unsupported. Their pain is recognized, but never answered. The wrong remains suspended, and so does the wound.

This is why judgment is not cruelty. It is solidarity with reality.

Judgment names what happened without dilution. It refuses to explain away harm. It places moral weight where it belongs—not on the victim's capacity to cope, but on the reality of the act itself.

And when judgment rests on solid ground, it does something unexpected.

It brings **rest**.

We have already seen the exhaustion of the internal courtroom—the endless trial where the judge keeps changing, the standards keep shifting, and the verdict is never final. Life on sand produces perpetual litigation. Innocence must be defended repeatedly. Guilt must be managed continuously. Nothing is ever settled.

This is not freedom. It is permanent negotiation.

But when judgment rests on something solid—when a final word can be spoken—the trial ends.

Even a difficult verdict is better than endless uncertainty. Even a hard truth is more humane than a lifetime of ambiguity. Closure does not require that the outcome be pleasant; it requires that it be final.

Judgment, when grounded, does not crush the soul.

It quiets it.

It says that reality has been seen, named, and answered. That nothing has been ignored. That no weight remains suspended. That the court has adjourned.

And that is the rest people have been searching for all along.

The Collapse of Moral Seriousness

One of the clearest signs that justice has lost its footing is the way we now speak about it.

Moral language has not disappeared, but it has grown hesitant. Words like truth, justice, and responsibility are still used, yet rarely without qualification. Statements are softened. Claims are hedged. Convictions are surrounded by disclaimers meant to signal humility, safety, or awareness.

This carefulness is often praised as maturity.

But something else is happening.

Modern moral speech exists in a kind of linguistic fog. Every assertion is followed by clarifications, caveats, and apologies—not simply out of politeness, but out of uncertainty. People are no longer sure the ground beneath a clear statement will hold. To speak plainly feels risky. To name wrong without buffering it feels dangerous.

So we circle the truth rather than standing on it.

This is not just a change in etiquette; it is a symptom of instability. When there is no solid foundation for judgment, moral language must remain indirect. Precision feels threatening. Certainty feels arrogant. Clarity feels like exposure.

The result is a culture that talks constantly about justice, but struggles to say what it is.

From this fog, cynicism is born.

When judgment is consistently framed as a power play, when moral claims are treated as psychological crutches or tools of control, trust evaporates. If every assertion of right and wrong is suspected of hidden motive, then sincerity itself becomes implausible.

No one is really believed.

No one is really innocent.

No one is really accountable.

This breeds a deep, corrosive suspicion—not only of institutions, but of one another. Moral concern is reinterpreted as manipulation. Conviction is reduced to strategy. Appeals to justice are met with eye-rolls rather than engagement.

Over time, outrage itself becomes exhausting.

Each week brings a new moral emergency. Each demands immediate response, full emotional investment, and public alignment. Yet few lead to resolution. The cycle repeats without closure. People are called to care deeply, again and again, without ever seeing justice settle.

Eventually, many stop responding.

Not because they are cruel, but because they are tired. Tired of standing on ground that shifts beneath every step. Tired of investing moral energy that never results in rest. Tired of outrage that flares brightly and then evaporates without meaningfully changing anything.

Apathy is not the opposite of moral seriousness.

It is often the casualty of its collapse.

This instability also produces a paradoxical brittleness.

Removing a foundation for justice does not make society kinder. It makes it fragile. On solid ground, disagreement can be endured because the foundation is not at risk. There is room for patience, for mercy, even for disagreement—because the truth does not depend on unanimous approval.

Where to Stand

On sand, every disagreement feels **existential**.

If there is no stable standard beneath us, then every challenge threatens collapse. This produces a culture that is soft on objective standards but harsh toward individuals. Rules become flexible, but enforcement becomes personal. Principles are negotiable, but deviation is punished swiftly.

The system appears tolerant, but the people within it feel constantly watched.

Finally, where truth loses authority, power fills the gap.

On shifting ground, justice becomes whatever the loudest voice can sustain. Visibility replaces virtue. Influence substitutes for innocence. Judgment does not disappear—it concentrates.

The will of the majority becomes the measure of right. The whim of the crowd becomes the verdict. Those with platforms are protected; those without them are exposed. The quiet, the weak, and the obscure find themselves without recourse, because justice now follows attention rather than truth.

This is judgment redistributed unevenly.

In such a world, seriousness collapses—not because people no longer care about right and wrong, but because there is no place left for those concepts to stand. Without ground, justice cannot settle. Without settlement, language erodes. Without language, trust dissolves.

What remains is noise, fatigue, and fragility.

And beneath it all, the unresolved weight of justice still presses—waiting for something solid enough to hold it.

The Question Sharpens

At this point, the problem can no longer be softened.

Justice is not merely a feeling. It is not an emotional response to harm, nor a social preference shaped by consensus. It behaves like something more solid than that—something that presses, insists, and refuses to be dismissed.

Justice feels true even when it is inconvenient.

It demands reckoning even when no one benefits from naming it.

It lingers even when every attempt has been made to explain it away.

Which suggests something unsettling.

If justice is more than a feeling—if it carries weight, if it demands answer, if it refuses to disappear—then reality itself must be capable of a reckoning. There must be something in the structure of the world that corresponds to this demand. Justice must have somewhere to stand.

Otherwise, outrage is an illusion.

Forgiveness is sentimentality.

Judgment is oppression.

And moral seriousness is a shared fiction we maintain until it becomes too exhausting to uphold.

But that explanation does not fit our experience.

We do not merely prefer justice. We expect it. We recognize its absence. We feel its violation as something objectively wrong, not merely subjectively painful. And we grow weary not because justice asks too much—but because it asks for something we have not yet found.

This is where all the threads of this chapter converge.

Justice cannot float.

Forgiveness cannot carry weight on sand.

Judgment cannot resolve without authority.

Responsibility cannot restore dignity without truth.

The demand remains. The ground does not.

And so the question sharpens—not as speculation, but as necessity:

Where can justice actually stand?

That question does not ask for a preference.

It does not invite a theory.

It demands a location.

Until that ground is found, the weight of justice will continue to press—on individuals, on cultures, on history itself—without relief.

Part II begins where this chapter must end.

Not with an answer offered lightly,

but with the possibility that the ground we have been standing on

was never meant to carry this weight at all.

Summary

This chapter has argued that justice is not a cultural preference, an emotional reaction, or a social construction that can be negotiated away. It is a demand that presses in on human life with undeniable weight.

Outrage proves its inescapability. Even in a pluralistic age, even among those who deny objective morality, the moment injustice is encountered, certainty erupts. Wrong is named instinctively, not academically. This demand cannot be silenced—it can only be displaced. And when it has nowhere solid to stand, it turns inward, trapping individuals and societies in an exhausting, unresolved courtroom.

Justice without judgment cannot heal. Affirmation without accountability leaves moral air thick with tension. Performative justice multiplies gestures but settles nothing. Compassion that replaces judgment obscures harm rather than answering it. Sand does not absorb guilt; it merely shifts it, scattering resentment and fatigue across relationships and cultures.

Forgiveness fares no better on unstable ground. Calls to "let go" ring hollow when the weight of wrong has nowhere to go. Cheap forgiveness denies reality rather than healing it. True forgiveness requires that the full moral weight of an offense be carried somewhere solid—something capable of bearing what the victim was never meant to hold alone.

Judgment, far from being cruelty, emerges as a moral necessity. To be judged is to be taken seriously as a moral agent. Without judgment, human actions become weightless, victims are left without vindication, and justice is redistributed to the crowd or the powerful. The result is not mercy, but brittleness: a society soft on standards yet harsh toward individuals, loud with outrage yet starved for resolution.

As justice loses its footing, moral seriousness collapses. Language grows hesitant. Conviction dissolves into caveats. Cynicism replaces trust. Outrage exhausts itself into apathy. Power fills the gap where truth once stood. None of this happens because people care less about justice, but because they are standing on ground that cannot hold its weight.

The chapter closes with an unavoidable conclusion: justice behaves like something real. It demands reckoning, insists on truth, and refuses to disappear. If justice is more than a feeling, then reality itself must be capable of answering it.

Which sharpens the question beyond abstraction:

Where can justice actually stand?

That question cannot be resolved on sand.

And until it is answered, the weight of justice will continue to press—without rest, without closure, and without peace.

Application: Questions of Ground

1. When you encounter injustice, what do you instinctively want to happen?

2. How do you respond to the idea of judgment—relief, resistance, fear, or confusion? Why?

3. Have you ever been asked to forgive without justice? What did that cost you?

4. Where do you see moral outrage today without meaningful resolution?

5. What would it require for justice to actually settle rather than cycle endlessly?

6. If justice is necessary, what kind of ground would it require?

Where to Stand

4

Why We Keep Sinking

The Instinct to Fix What Is Failing

When something is failing beneath us, the first response is almost always the same: fix it.

This instinct is not foolish. It is human. When the ground feels unstable, we look for ways to reinforce it —new habits, better tools, clearer systems. We assume the problem lies not with where we are standing, but with how well we are standing there.

This instinct explains the modern fatigue surrounding self-improvement.

Ours is an age of optimization. Apps promise clarity. Journals promise focus. Therapy-speak promises insight and healing. Each tool offers something real. Many of them are genuinely helpful. They can improve communication, regulate emotion, and bring awareness to patterns that would otherwise remain hidden.

But these tools are increasingly being asked to do work they were never designed to do.

They are being used to reinforce the sand.

Instead of supporting life on solid ground, they are pressed into service as foundations themselves. We do not ask them merely to assist us—we ask them to stabilize us. To hold identity together. To bear the weight of guilt, purpose, and meaning.

The result is exhaustion.

No matter how refined the strategy, no amount of optimization can make shifting ground hold still. A better routine can improve the experience of instability, but it cannot remove it. A clearer self-understanding can explain why the sand shifts, but it cannot stop the movement.

The problem is not effort.

It is placement.

A similar trap appears in religious effort.

When the ground feels unstable, sincerity becomes a substitute for solidity. People pray harder, serve longer, confess more frequently, and discipline themselves more strictly—not because these things are wrong, but because they are being used to thicken the sand.

Religious activity becomes reinforcement rather than response.

The assumption is subtle but powerful: If I am sincere enough, committed enough, obedient enough, then the ground will eventually hold. Faith becomes another technique. Devotion becomes another lever. God becomes another resource for stabilization rather than the One who provides ground.

This is why religious effort so often intensifies guilt instead of relieving it.

The harder one tries to be good on unstable ground, the more aware one becomes of failure. The sand does not forgive effort; it absorbs it. Every step sinks slightly deeper. Every attempt to pull upward increases the sense of instability.

Sincerity cannot substitute for solidity.

This brings us back to the image of the miry pit.

Sand behaves differently under pressure. When you struggle against it, it tightens. When you pull upward, it grips downward. The instinct to fight the ground only gives the ground more control. What feels like resistance becomes entrapment.

This is why so many people who are genuinely trying to live well feel increasingly unstable.

They are not lazy.

They are not indifferent.

They are not careless.

They are pulling against sand.

The harder they try to be good, the more the sand claims them. Guilt deepens. Anxiety sharpens. Identity feels less secure, not more. What began as effort turns into panic. What began as responsibility turns into despair.

The pit is not exposing moral failure—it is exposing structural failure.

This is the great tragedy of self-improvement and religious striving on unstable ground. The very instinct to fix what is failing becomes the mechanism by which the failure accelerates.

Not because effort is wrong.

But because sand cannot be reinforced.

And the more earnestly we try to make it solid, the more clearly it reveals that it never was.

One of the clearest illustrations of this pattern comes not from modern self-help culture, but from a man who took moral seriousness to its extreme. Long before he became a reformer, Martin Luther was a monk consumed by the need to be right with God. He spent hours in confession, retracing his thoughts, motives, and impulses, terrified that one overlooked sin might condemn him. He fasted, prayed, deprived himself of sleep, and disciplined his body relentlessly —not out of rebellion, but sincerity. Yet the harder he tried, the more unstable he felt. Guilt did not lift; it deepened. Assurance did not come; anxiety intensified. Luther was not failing to care. He was failing to find ground. His effort did not quiet his conscience—it sharpened it. What he discovered, painfully and slowly, was that sincerity could exhaust the soul without ever stabilizing it. The sand did not hold, no matter how earnestly he pressed into it.

The Logic of the Miry Pit

The tragedy of the miry pit is not that it traps careless people.

It traps strivers.

A pit of mud or sand behaves differently than solid ground. On firm soil, effort produces movement.

Where to Stand

When you push, the ground pushes back. Energy transfers upward. Growth follows strain.

But the miry pit obeys a different logic.

In unstable ground, effort creates suction.

When a person senses moral instability—guilt that will not settle, identity that feels fragile, standing that feels uncertain—the instinct is to pull upward. We exert willpower. We resolve to do better. We rehearse our intentions. We attempt to lift ourselves out through effort, discipline, or performance.

But that pull creates a vacuum.

The very act of trying to extract oneself tightens the surrounding ground. Sand rushes in to fill the space. Weight settles. Resistance increases. What feels like determination becomes entrapment.

This is the moral vacuum.

When the self becomes both the problem and the solution, every attempt to rise deepens self-reference. Attention collapses inward. Past failures gain gravity. Memory presses down. The harder one tries to prove goodness, the more the unresolved weight of what has already been done settles around the ankles.

This is not weakness.

It is mechanics.

There is a crucial difference between healthy effort and miry effort.

Healthy effort assumes solid ground. It moves outward. It builds, serves, learns, and grows. When it fails, the ground remains. Failure instructs rather than condemns. Repentance leads to restoration. Movement is possible because footing is secure.

Miry effort is different.

Miry effort is effort directed toward justification. It is thrashing meant to demonstrate worth. It is performance offered as proof of standing. Because the ground is unstable, effort must now do double duty: not only accomplishing good, but securing identity.

That burden is too heavy.

The more one strives to show that they are a good person, the more the past asserts itself. The mind replays missteps. Motives are scrutinized. The self becomes a courtroom again—evidence piling up faster than it can be answered.

The pit responds predictably.

Each motion pulls more sand inward. Each attempt to rise sinks the body further. The person does not become freer; they become more conscious of their inability to stand.

This is why moral striving so often leads not to confidence, but to anxiety. Not to clarity, but to collapse. The effort itself becomes evidence that something is wrong—not with desire, but with location.

The pit does not expose laziness.

It exposes misplaced effort.

The sand does not resist because you are unworthy.

It resists because it cannot be stood upon.

This is the logic of the miry pit:

> *Effort without ground becomes entanglement,*

> *and sincerity without solidity becomes descent.*

The harder you pull, the deeper you feel the weight.

Not because you are beyond rescue,

but because rescue cannot come from within the pit itself.

When Improvement Makes Things Worse

One of the most confusing experiences in modern moral life is this:

The more seriously a person takes goodness, the worse they often feel.

This is not because improvement fails to occur. In many cases, real growth is happening. Habits change. Behaviors improve. Awareness deepens. And yet, instead of relief, there is increased tension— greater guilt, sharper anxiety, a growing sense that the distance between who one is and who one ought to be is widening rather than closing.

This is the paradox of awareness.

Moral seriousness sharpens moral eyesight. As a person grows, they begin to notice flaws they once ignored. Motives become visible. Half-measures feel dishonest. What once passed unnoticed now presses on the conscience. The standard rises, not because it has changed, but because the person can finally see it.

> On solid ground, this clarity produces humility and growth.

> On sand, it produces despair.

Imagine someone trying to clean a room whose floor rests on unstable ground. They scrub harder. They work more carefully. But every time they clean the surface, more dirt seeps up from beneath the boards. The cleaner they try to make the room, the clearer it becomes that the problem is not the mess—it is the floor itself.

Improvement does not solve the problem.

It exposes it.

This is the difference between growth and standing.

Growth is a change in the person.

Standing is a change in the ground.

Improvement can refine posture, behavior, and intention—but it cannot stabilize what lies beneath. If you are standing in mud, standing up straighter does not stop the sinking. In fact, it often makes it worse. A more upright stance concentrates weight. The footprint deepens. Collapse accelerates.

This is why self-repair on unstable ground feels like betrayal.

The effort is sincere.

The intention is good.

The result is greater instability.

Nowhere is this more evident than in religious effort.

Spiritual disciplines—prayer, study, service, confession—are good things. They are meant to shape love, deepen trust, and orient life toward God. But when they are used as tools for stabilization—

ways to earn footing rather than respond to grace—they become heavier reinforcements laid on sand.

Religiosity is not the rejection of God.

It is the attempt to use God to fix the ground.

The result is often a more sensitive conscience without greater rest. Moral perception becomes refined. The person sees sin more clearly, desires holiness more earnestly, and therefore feels failure more acutely. The inner courtroom becomes more sophisticated, not quieter.

Religious sincerity, when misdirected, does not calm the soul.

It trains it to manage righteousness.

And management is exhausting.

A "better" self is often a heavier self. Higher values, deeper convictions, and greater moral sensitivity add weight. There is more to protect, more to justify, more to lose. When the foundation is unstable, this increased weight makes collapse more likely, not less.

This is why improvement that does not free is such a common experience.

People are not becoming worse.

They are becoming more serious.

But seriousness without ground intensifies the problem it is trying to solve. The sand cannot carry the weight of a sharpened conscience. The more valuable the structure, the more catastrophic the failure when the foundation gives way.

Improvement was never meant to bear this burden.

It was never meant to provide standing.

And when it is asked to do so, it does not deliver stability—it reveals, with painful clarity, that something deeper must change.

The Bankruptcy of Values

One of the reasons instability persists is that values can imitate solidity for a very long time. But this imitation rests on a distinction that often goes unspoken and rarely examined.

Values are negotiated.

Virtues are established.

Values arise from agreement—personal, cultural, or communal. They reflect what a group decides to prize, reward, or protect. Because they are formed by consensus, they remain flexible. They can be refined, updated, or replaced as circumstances change. Their authority extends only as far as the agreement that sustains them.

Virtues are different. They are not voted into existence. They do not depend on approval, visibility, or performance. Virtues are rooted in an authority beyond the self—an order of reality that does not shift when opinion does. They describe what is good whether it is rewarded or ignored, celebrated or punished.

This difference matters the moment pressure arrives.

A person can possess an impressive moral life—clear commitments, strong convictions, years of sacrifice and service—and still lack anything capable of bearing weight. By most outward measures, they appear secure. Their conscience feels funded. Their standing seems established.

But moral life, like financial life, has more than one metric.

A person may have a high moral net worth and still lack liquidity. On paper, the assets are there. The résumé is strong. The values are affirmed. Yet when a crisis comes—deep guilt, moral failure, suffering that cannot be explained—the question is not how much has been accumulated over time. The question is whether anything can bear weight now.

This is where many discover that their values cannot be cashed in.

History offers a striking parallel. For a time, wampum functioned as currency in early colonial America. It worked because everyone agreed it worked. It circulated. It purchased goods. It symbolized value. But wampum had no intrinsic weight; it depended entirely on shared consent. When economic systems shifted and stronger currency entered the market, its value collapsed almost overnight.

Not because it was imaginary—but because it lacked authority.

Values on sand function the same way. They circulate socially. They signal belonging. They purchase legitimacy, approval, and self-respect. But when reality performs an audit—when loss occurs, when sin surfaces, when death or injustice presses hard—they cannot be exchanged for stability.

Moments of collapse become a run on the bank of the soul. We go to the vault of good intentions, past sacrifices, and moral commitments, hoping to find comfort or standing there. But under pressure, the vault is empty.

The values were never gold.

They were currency printed by agreement on shifting ground.

This is not because values are meaningless. It is because they were never meant to be security. They express what we love; they cannot hold us when weight is applied.

Virtues, by contrast, are not spent. They are revealed.

On solid ground, virtues are the fruit of security. They grow outward from a place of standing rather than being used to purchase it. Failure may wound, but it does not bankrupt. Repentance deepens rather than destabilizes. A person can grieve their sin without losing their footing.

On sand, values become the price of existence.

They must be performed continually. They must be updated as standards shift. They must be defended when challenged. When you fail to live up to them, you do not merely feel regret—you lose standing. The account dips. Anxiety rises. You are not asking whether something was right, but whether you are still acceptable.

This is how values become burdens rather than guides.

On shifting ground, the price of feeling like a good person keeps rising. New causes demand allegiance. New vocabularies signal virtue. New rituals of belonging must be performed. Yesterday's righteousness becomes today's negligence. Moral inflation sets in.

You work harder, but the returns diminish. The same effort buys less peace. The same commitments secure less rest. To remain solvent, you must adopt new standards and demonstrate alignment more visibly. The books are never balanced for long.

This is not moral growth.

It is moral survival.

And survival is exhausting when the currency itself is unstable.

The irony is that this process often looks like seriousness. In reality, it is fragility. The self becomes dependent on constant validation because it has no place to stand when validation falters. Values that were meant to point beyond the self now orbit it endlessly.

Here is the counterintuitive truth: the realization of bankruptcy—painful as it is—can become a **gift**.

As long as you believe you have just enough value to keep standing, you will keep fixing the books. You will reinterpret losses, justify deficits, and convince yourself that solvency is only one more effort away. Helpless autonomy persists as long as hope remains in self-issued credit.

Bankruptcy ends the illusion.

It exposes what was already true: no amount of moral accounting can secure standing on sand. The problem is not poor management; it is misplaced trust. The books cannot be balanced because the ground beneath them is unstable.

This is the mercy of the end.

When the vault is empty, the search finally changes direction. You stop trying to prove worth and begin asking where standing actually comes from. You stop reinforcing the sand and begin to wonder whether something solid exists beneath it.

That question does not yet have an answer here.

But bankruptcy clears the way for it.

And that clearing—humiliating, painful, and honest—is often the first moment real freedom becomes possible.

The Audit We Cannot Avoid

Eventually, every system faces an audit.

There is a difference between a storm and an audit. A storm is something that happens to us. It arrives uninvited, disrupts our plans, and tests our endurance. Storms may injure, frighten, or exhaust us, but they do not ask questions. They can sometimes be endured through sheer grit. People survive storms by holding on.

An audit is different. An audit is not an event that strikes us from the outside; it is an inquiry into what we have built. It does not ask how hard we tried or how sincere our intentions were. It does not respond to effort or resilience. An audit simply examines whether anything present can actually bear weight.

And no one grits their way through an audit.

Crises often function this way. A moral failure that can no longer be hidden. The collapse of a reputation. The quiet approach of death. These moments act like a cosmic auditor. They are not impressed by our forged paths or our carefully curated narratives. They do not negotiate. They ask one question and refuse to move on until it is answered:

Is there anything here that can actually hold?

This is why audits feel so different from suffering alone. Suffering hurts, but an audit exposes. It searches beneath appearances. It tests foundations rather than intentions. And it does not care how long something has stood if it was never anchored.

Those who live on sand often fear the public audit most. They dread exposure, shame, loss of standing, or being judged by the crowd. Public failure feels catastrophic because so much has been invested in appearing stable. A public audit threatens identity itself.

But the most devastating audit is rarely the public one.

It is the private audit.

It arrives in the quiet hours, when distractions fade and explanations lose their force. At three in the morning, when no one is watching, the books are opened. The questions cannot be postponed. The inner courtroom from Chapter 2 reappears—but something has changed.

You are no longer the only one present. In the audit, a third party enters: reality.

Reality cannot be bribed with self-justification. It cannot be managed with negotiated misery. It does not respond to sincerity or effort. It simply reveals what is there. The ledgers are examined. The numbers are run. And slowly, unmistakably, it becomes clear that the accounts do not balance.

This is where the illusion of moral equity collapses.

Many people live as though they have built up credit with God, with the universe, or with life itself. Good deeds are accumulated. Sacrifices are logged. Suffering endured is treated as investment. The assumption is quiet but powerful: I have earned standing.

The audit reveals something else.

The problem was never the effort. The problem was the land. The property was built on ground that was never owned. Autonomy felt like ownership, but it was only occupancy. The structure may have looked impressive, but there was no title to the ground beneath it.

This is where the map analogy comes into focus. We believed we were forging our own path, building something meaningful along the way. The audit shows that we were navigating dunes, not roads— constructing a mansion on terrain that could not be claimed or secured. The failure is not moral incompetence; it is misplaced confidence.

The audit is not punishment.

It is disclosure.

It reveals that the foundation was never solid, that the ground was never ours, and that no amount of effort could change that fact. What collapses is not goodness, but the illusion that goodness could function as ground.

And here, unexpectedly, the audit becomes mercy.

If the sand never failed, we would remain on it until it was too late. We would keep reinforcing what cannot hold, mistaking effort for security and sincerity for solidity. The audit interrupts that trajectory. It issues a final notice: This building is condemned.

Not to destroy us—but to force us to look for another home.

This is the moment when helpless autonomy is finally revealed as a burden rather than a freedom. The constant managing, justifying, and stabilizing is exposed as unsustainable. The self, exhausted from holding everything together, is finally allowed to stop pretending it can.

Only then are we ready to hear an invitation that does not ask for effort, explanation, or proof—but for rest.

The audit clears the ground.

And once the ground is cleared, the possibility of standing somewhere else can finally be heard.

Struggle or Stillness

There is a moment in every true crisis when the struggle stops—not because the problem is solved, but because the options have run out.

In physical quicksand, rescue begins only when the person stops thrashing. Stillness is not a technique. It is the collapse of false solutions. It is the realization that autonomy has reached its limit.

The same is true here.

This stillness is not virtue. It is not merit. It is not a final contribution. It is the end of pretending that the ground beneath us can be made to hold by effort or sincerity.

It is the admission, often unspoken but unmistakable: I cannot stand on my own ground.

Why Only Relocation Can Save

At this point, the logic becomes unavoidable.

If the problem were effort, more effort would solve it.

If the problem were knowledge, clarity would fix it.

If the problem were discipline, resolve would overcome it.

But the problem is location.

You cannot stand where standing is impossible. You cannot stabilize yourself where the ground itself is unstable. And you cannot move yourself to solid ground by struggling against the very conditions that are pulling you under.

If rescue is possible, it must come from outside the pit. It must involve being lifted, not improved—placed, not perfected.

It must be **relocation**.

Why This Is Not Defeat

To admit this feels like failure. But it is not failure—it is truth.

As long as the struggle continues, rescue is impossible. As long as autonomy is defended, solid ground cannot be received. The end of effort is not despair; it is the only point at which help becomes intelligible.

This is not an emotional breakthrough. It is a structural one.

Summary

This chapter has shown why self-repair fails not because people lack sincerity or effort, but because effort applied to unstable ground deepens the problem. Like quicksand, the struggle itself creates the vacuum that pulls a person under.

Values function as a local moral currency, adding weight without purchasing stability. Improvement sharpens awareness but cannot resolve guilt. The result is not immorality, but bankruptcy.

When all internal strategies fail, the only remaining possibility is rescue from outside the system. Stability, if it exists, cannot be achieved. It must be received.

Application: Questions of Ground

1. Where have your most sincere efforts failed to bring lasting stability?

2. Have improvement and awareness ever increased your sense of moral weight rather than relieved it?

3. What "values" feel most important to you—and where do they fail under pressure?

4. How do you respond when effort no longer works: more struggle, distraction, or stillness?

5. What would it mean to admit that the problem is not effort, but location?

6. If solid ground exists, what would it require for you to be placed there rather than climb there?

II

The Rock Revealed

Where to Stand

5

The Rock Beneath the Sand

When Rescue Becomes Thinkable

By the end of the last chapter, one conclusion has become unavoidable: if stability exists, it cannot be achieved by effort. The struggle itself has been exposed as part of the problem. The question is no longer how to fix ourselves, but whether solid ground exists at all.

That question does not arise in moments of comfort. It emerges only when every internal strategy has failed. When effort is exhausted, when moral currency is spent, and when the self finally runs out of ways to manage instability, the possibility of rescue becomes thinkable for the first time.

This is not optimism. It is **realism**.

Up to this point, the dominant assumption has been that stability must come from within—from better effort, clearer understanding, or stronger resolve. Chapter after chapter has shown why that assumption fails. Effort deepens the pit. Improvement increases awareness without relieving guilt. Values accumulate weight without providing ground. The audit reveals not a lack of sincerity, but a lack of standing.

Eventually, something else happens.

The struggle stops.

Not because the problem has been solved, but because the options have been exhausted. The thrashing that once felt necessary is recognized as futile. What remains is not confidence or clarity, but stillness. This stillness is not virtue. It is not humility performed well. It is not a final contribution offered to earn rescue. It is the quiet admission that the ground beneath us cannot be made to hold.

At this point, rescue no longer sounds like defeat.

As long as autonomy is defended, help remains unintelligible. Rescue feels like surrender because it threatens the last illusion of control. But when autonomy collapses under its own weight, rescue becomes conceivable—not because strength has returned, but because pretense has ended.

This is why Jesus begins not with instruction, but with blessing: "Blessed are the poor in spirit: for theirs is the kingdom of heaven" (Matthew 5:3, KJV). To be poor in spirit is not to lack moral concern. It is to lack moral capital. It is to stand before reality without leverage, without reserve, and without the resources to justify oneself.

In the logic of the sand, this condition is failure. It is exposure. It is the end of standing.

But in the logic of the Rock, this is the threshold.

Only those who know they cannot stand on their own ground are capable of being placed on another. Only when bankruptcy is acknowledged does rescue stop sounding abstract or unnecessary. The end of effort does not produce despair; it creates the first space where help can be received.

Rescue becomes thinkable not when we discover new strength, but when we finally stop pretending we have any.

A Name for the Pit

Up to this point, the miry pit has been described as an experience—an exhaustion, a collapse, a stillness that follows the failure of effort. But Scripture does not leave this condition unnamed. It does not treat it as a vague psychological hurdle or a temporary emotional low. It gives it a name, and in doing so, it gives us clarity we may not initially welcome.

Before the pit can be escaped, it must be understood.

We often imagine ourselves as lost travelers—well-intentioned, disoriented, doing our best with limited information. But Scripture describes something more precise. The human heart is not merely lost; it is willful. It is not just wandering; it is choosing.

A better image is not the lost traveler, but the rebellious surveyor.

God has not left humanity without direction. The map was provided. The path was marked. The ground that could bear weight was not hidden. But when we examined the way laid out for us, we found it too narrow, too restrictive, too confining to our sense of independence. We folded the map, not because it was unclear, but because we did not want to walk where it led.

So we decided to forge our own path across the dunes.

This matters because the heart, in Scripture, is not primarily the seat of emotion, but of will. It is the place where decisions are made, where allegiance is chosen, and where authority is either acknowledged or rejected. The pit is not merely something that happened to us; it is the result of where we insisted on standing.

Culpability lies not in the existence of the pit, but in the refusal of the path.

This is why Scripture speaks with such unsettling precision. "He brought me up also out of an horrible pit, out of the miry clay" (Psalm 40:2, KJV). The Psalmist does not describe a mild inconvenience or a passing struggle. The phrase translated "horrible pit" carries the sense of noise, tumult, and chaos—a pit of roaring confusion.

This detail matters.

The pit is not silent. It is loud. It is the place where competing justifications collide, where accusations—both internal and external—echo constantly. It is the Internal Courtroom you encountered earlier, amplified by the judgment of the crowd and the pressure of self-defense. The noise is so constant that truth becomes difficult to hear at all.

This is not merely emotional distress. It is **moral disorientation**.

Scripture names this condition with a word that has been flattened by overuse: **sin**. But sin, in its most basic biblical sense, does not begin as a list of mistakes. It is described as *"missing the mark."* And the mark is not abstract. The mark is a life that stands —one that bears weight, endures judgment, and remains grounded under reality.

If the only place that mark can be hit is from solid ground, then choosing the sand makes missing inevitable.

This is the crucial insight: our failure is not primarily about poor aim, but about poor placement. We are culpable not because we failed despite standing on the Rock, but because we refused the Rock and insisted on standing elsewhere. Sin is the pride that says, *I can hit the mark while standing on my own terms.*

The physics of the pit reinforce this truth. Autonomy is not neutral space; it creates a vacuum. The more fiercely we insist on independence, the more the ground gives way beneath us. The harder we thrash to establish self-made stability, the deeper we sink. What feels like freedom accelerates collapse.

Sin, then, is not merely wrongdoing. It is the refusal of dependence on the only ground that does not shift. It is the sustained attempt to generate weight from a self that was never meant to bear it.

And until the pit is named honestly—until we recognize that it is not only tragic but chosen—rescue will remain confusing, offensive, or unnecessary.

But once the name is spoken, something else becomes possible.

The Rock That Precedes the Rescue

When people imagine rescue, they usually picture interruption. Something goes wrong, help arrives, danger is removed, and life resumes. The emphasis is on timing and urgency—getting someone out before it's too late.

That image makes sense in emergencies, but it quietly assumes something else: that once the danger is escaped, there will be somewhere safe to stand.

In a world with real weight, that assumption matters.

If guilt is more than a feeling, if injustice is more than opinion, if loss and death are more than unfortunate interruptions, then rescue cannot simply be an extraction. It cannot hover above reality or bypass it. Whatever rescues a person must also be capable of receiving what they carry afterward. Otherwise, relief may be felt, but stability will not follow.

This helps explain a common experience. Many people describe moments of clarity, resolve, or even relief—times when something seemed to lift, when the pressure eased. But the effect rarely lasts. Life settles back into strain. The same anxieties return. The same effort is required just to stay upright.

The problem is not sincerity. It is sequence.

Rescue that comes before solid ground can only be temporary. Without a place that can bear weight, rescue becomes a pause rather than a relocation. The danger is interrupted, but nothing changes underneath.

This is where the metaphor of ground becomes unavoidable.

Sand can absorb movement. It can cushion impact. It can even hide what we would rather not see. But it cannot hold. Anything placed on it must be continually adjusted to remain upright. Over time, the effort required simply to stand consumes the energy that might otherwise be used to live.

If rescue leaves a person standing on the same shifting surface, the result is predictable. They are grateful—but still bracing. Relieved—but still exhausted. Help has come, but nothing has settled.

So the more basic question is not how rescue happens, **but whether there is any ground capable of making rescue meaningful.**

If such ground exists, it must come first. It must already be there—unmoved by the weight that overwhelms us. It cannot be created by effort or summoned by need. It must be discovered, not constructed.

Only then does rescue make sense—not as escape from reality, but as placement within it. Not as avoidance of weight, but as transfer onto something that can finally receive it.

This also reframes what rescue would look like if it were real. It would not primarily feel dramatic. It would feel quiet. Like the first moment when the ground beneath your feet stops shifting and you realize you no longer need to keep adjusting your balance. The danger may not yet be explained. The cost may not yet be understood. But the difference is unmistakable: something is holding that wasn't holding before.

If such ground exists, it would not be a new invention or a clever solution. It would not be the result of cultural progress or personal insight. Ground that can bear this kind of weight cannot be manufactured on demand.

It would have to be revealed—noticed only when the sand gives way enough for something solid to be felt beneath it.

That possibility raises the next question:

If this ground is real, why does it feel both unfamiliar and strangely recognizable?

Not a New Idea, but a Revealed One

This is where many misunderstand the Christian claim. Christianity does not argue that belief creates reality. It argues that belief recognizes reality.

The rock is not a comforting idea projected onto chaos. It is described as the underlying order of things—what holds when everything else gives way. It is not discovered through effort, but revealed when effort fails.

This is why the language of *revelation* matters. The rock is not assembled from fragments of human wisdom. It is disclosed. Seen. Recognized.

In other words, the answer to instability is not innovation, but **illumination**.

When the Ground Has a Face

Up to this point, the discussion has remained abstract —ground, sand, rock. But the biblical claim is more specific. The rock is not merely a principle or a force. It is personal.

This is the moment where the argument becomes concrete.

The Scriptures identify the rock as the God who made the world and entered it—not as an idea, but as a person. The ground that holds is not an impersonal standard, but a living reality capable of bearing weight because it stands independent of human effort.

This is not yet an explanation of how rescue happens. It is the recognition that rescue has an address.

Why the Rock Must Enter the Sand

- If the problem were ignorance, instruction would be enough.

- If the problem were weakness, assistance would suffice.

- If the problem were confusion, clarity would resolve it.

But the problem is location.

Those trapped in the pit cannot climb out without deepening the trap. Solid ground cannot be reached from below. If rescue is to occur, the rock must do something unexpected: it must come near.

The Scriptures describe this movement with startling restraint. God does not shout instructions from above the pit. He enters the human condition—stepping into the instability, the weight, the consequences—without becoming unstable Himself.

This is not sentiment. It is necessity.

The Weight the Rock Can Bear

What qualifies the rock as solid is not its appearance, but its capacity. It must be able to bear weight—real weight. Moral weight. Human guilt. The accumulated pressure of injustice and death.

Anything less would fracture.

Most things that appear stable fail precisely here. They hold under ordinary conditions but give way when pressed. They manage everyday strain but collapse when asked to carry more than comfort or coherence. The surface may look firm. The language may sound convincing. But weight reveals what appearance cannot.

This is why the question of capacity matters more than description.

Guilt, for example, is not merely a feeling that can be processed or released. It is a claim. It presses for acknowledgment. It demands reckoning. When it is ignored or reframed, it does not disappear; it waits. What cannot bear it must either deny it or deflect it. Both strategies reduce pressure temporarily, but neither resolves it.

The same is true of injustice. Injustice accumulates. It does not dissolve with time or explanation. It presses forward, asking not only to be noticed, but to be answered. Systems built on negotiation or consensus can delay that pressure, but they cannot absorb it. Eventually, something gives—either truth is thinned, or outrage multiplies.

Death is the heaviest weight of all. It is not simply an event but a finality. It refuses reinterpretation. It does not negotiate with meaning or yield to optimism. Any ground that cannot face it directly is exposed as provisional. Whatever fractures here was never solid to begin with.

This is the test the rock must pass.

The claim the Scriptures make is that the rock does not crack under this weight. It does not shift. It does not absorb guilt by ignoring it. It holds.

That claim is deliberately severe. It does not say the weight is reduced. It does not say the burden is softened. It says the weight is borne. What presses down does not vanish; it is received without collapse.

This claim is not yet explained here. It is stated because it must be.

Without it, the rock would be no different from the sand.

Sand can manage appearance. It can rearrange itself to accommodate pressure. It can make collapse gradual rather than sudden. But it cannot carry judgment, settle injustice, or face death without giving way. Any foundation that must reinterpret weight in order to survive has already failed the test.

So the difference between sand and rock is not intensity, sincerity, or effort. It is capacity. One shifts under pressure; the other remains. One survives by adjustment; the other by strength.

If such a rock exists—one that can bear the full weight of human reality without cracking—then it cannot be a recent discovery or a fragile insight. Ground capable of this kind of endurance does not emerge from cultural progress or personal reflection.

It would have to be older than our explanations. Deeper than our systems. Present before our attempts to name it.

Standing Before Understanding

At this stage, many want explanation. They want mechanics. They want to know how relocation happens, what it requires, and what it means.

Those questions matter. They will be addressed.

But before explanation comes recognition. Before understanding comes standing.

The invitation here is not to believe yet, but to see. To consider the possibility that stability exists independent of effort, and that the ground beneath reality has been revealed rather than constructed.

We often imagine that we are missing the mark because the instructions were unclear. But biblical sin —*hamartia*—is more than a lack of information; it is a rejection of the only Ground that can hold us.

Imagine a map that clearly marks a narrow, stone path leading to the destination. It is the only solid footing in a world of liquid dunes. But we look at that path and find it too restrictive, too narrow, or perhaps too 'given.' No one we know is on that path. It is old, neglected, and not very attractive. In our autonomy, we decide to fold the map and forge our own way across the sand.

We choose the sand because we want to be the architects of our own progress. We want the credit for the journey. The culpability lies in the fact that we insist on standing where we were never meant to stand. We 'miss the mark' because we have abandoned the only foundation from which the mark can actually be reached. Our 'helplessness' is not a victimhood; it is the inevitable consequence of our pride. We have traded the Rock for a self-made path that reality refuses to support.

No One Starts on the Rock

It is important to name something plainly before we move on.

The sand is not merely a bad option some people choose. It is the ground we inherit. Long before we develop a philosophy, adopt a morality, or build a personal brand, we are already standing somewhere —and the "somewhere" is unstable. We don't arrive on sand because we took the wrong exit. We begin there. We learn its habits as normal. We build our lives around its shifting.

"The fool hath said in his heart, There is no God. They are corrupt, they have done abominable works, there is none that doeth good.

The LORD looked down from heaven upon the children of men, to see if there were any that did understand, and seek God.

They are all gone aside, they are all together become filthy: there is none that doeth good, no, not one."

(Psalm 14:1–3)

This is why the sand feels universal even when the stories differ. One person tries to stand on pleasure, another on achievement, another on reputation, another on control, another on being "right." But the difference is usually in strategy, not in ground. The surface varies; the foun-dation does not. However refined our reasons be-come, we are still trying to make weight rest on something that cannot hold it.

Scripture does not treat this as a modern crisis or a cultural phase. It treats it as a human condition—shared, pervasive, and deeply rooted. Not simply that people do wrong things, but that the ground beneath the human heart is already tilted away from God and therefore unable to stand cleanly before Him.

The point is not to insult the reader. The point is to remove the illusion that anyone stands on stable ground by nature. If the sand were only a problem for the reckless, then the solution could be discipline. If the sand were only a problem for the uninformed, then the solution could be education. But if the sand is the shared human ground, then the solution cannot come from inside the sand.

And that is why the Rock —if it exists—cannot be reached by self-improvement. It cannot be achieved as a higher level of stability. It must be approached as relocation.

> "What then? are we better than they? No, in no wise: for we have before proved both Jews and Gentiles, that they are all under sin;
>
> As it is written, There is none righteous, no, not one:
>
> There is none that understandeth, there is none that seeketh after God.
>
> They are all gone out of the way, they are together become unprofitable; there is none that doeth good, no, not one. ...
>
> For all have sinned, and come short of the glory of God."
>
> (Romans 3:9–12, 23)

Being placed somewhere you did not build. Standing on ground you did not produce.

So the Rock is not the option for the especially religious. It is not the solution for the unusually guilty. It is not the upgrade for people who tried hard and failed.

It is the only ground that can hold anyone.

And that means whatever brings a person onto the Rock must be something stronger than willpower—stronger than clarity—stronger than resolve. It must be an act of rescue that does not merely interrupt the sinking, but moves the person to a different kind of ground altogether.

Summary

This chapter has introduced the possibility that solid ground exists and has always existed beneath the sand. The Scriptures describe this ground not as a concept, but as a rock capable of bearing weight and establishing those who stand upon it.

Rescue, if it is to occur, cannot originate from within the pit. It must involve being brought up and placed on ground that does not move. The rock precedes the rescue and makes it possible.

What remains to be seen is how this rock can bear the full weight of human guilt and justice without collapsing.

That question leads directly to what comes next.

Application: Questions of Ground

1. What makes the idea of solid ground feel necessary rather than merely comforting?

2. How does the idea of being placed differ from the idea of improving yourself?

3. Does the possibility that reality has a stable foundation feel hopeful, threatening, or both? Why?

4. What would it mean if truth and justice were not negotiated, but given?

5. If the rock exists independently of effort, what does that suggest about the nature of rescue?

Where to Stand

6

When the Weight Fell on the Rock

The Test No Ground Can Avoid

If solid ground truly exists, it must be able to bear weight. Not theoretical weight, but real weight—the kind that breaks systems, shatters explanations, and exposes foundations.

Weight reveals what holds and what does not.

Throughout history, ideas have promised stability only to collapse under pressure. Moral systems fracture when guilt accumulates. Political systems fail when justice becomes costly. Personal resolve gives way when suffering exceeds control. Sand always reveals itself eventually.

If the Rock described in the previous chapter is truly solid, it cannot be proven by words alone. It must be tested.

The cross is that test.

Guilt is not merely an emotion. It is moral weight—the accumulated reality of choices made, harm done, and responsibility borne. It does not disappear when ignored, nor is it erased by time. It presses downward, demanding resolution. Any ground that claims to hold reality must be able to deal with guilt honestly—without denial, evasion, or collapse.

The same is true of injustice. Injustice accumulates. It does not dissolve with explanation or apology. It presses forward, asking not only to be acknowledged, but to be answered. Systems built on negotiation or consensus can delay that pressure, but they cannot absorb it. Eventually, something gives—either truth is thinned, or outrage multiplies.

Death is the heaviest weight of all. It is not simply an event, but a finality. It refuses reinterpretation. It does not negotiate with meaning or yield to optimism. Any ground that cannot face death directly is exposed as provisional. Whatever fractures here was never solid to begin with.

This is the test the Rock must pass.

The claim Scripture makes is severe: the Rock does not crack under this weight. It does not shift. It does not absorb guilt by ignoring it. It holds.

It does not say the weight is reduced.

It does not say the burden is softened.

It says the weight is borne.

What presses down does not vanish; it is received without collapse.

Without this claim, the Rock would be no different from the sand.

Sand can manage appearance. It can rearrange itself to accommodate pressure. It can make collapse gradual rather than sudden. But it cannot carry judgment, settle injustice, or face death without giving way. Any foundation that must reinterpret weight in order to survive has already failed the test.

> *"Surely he hath borne our griefs, and carried our sorrows...*
>
> *the LORD hath laid on him the iniquity of us all."*
>
> *(Isaiah 53:4, 6)*
>
> *"Who his own self bare our sins in his own body on the tree."*
>
> *(1 Peter 2:24)*

So the difference between sand and rock is not intensity, sincerity, or effort. It is capacity. One shifts under pressure; the other remains. One survives by adjustment; the other by strength.

If such a Rock exists—one that can bear the full weight of human reality without cracking—then it cannot be a recent discovery or a fragile insight. Ground capable of this kind of endurance does not emerge from cultural progress or personal reflection. It would have to be older than our explanations, deeper than our systems, present before our attempts to name it.

At this stage, many want explanation. They want mechanics. They want to know how such bearing is possible.

Those questions matter. They will be addressed. But before explanation comes recognition. Before *understanding* comes *standing*.

The claim before us is not yet an invitation. It is a declaration about reality. Either the weight fell—and was held—or it did not. If it did not, then the Rock is no different from the sand, and the logic of collapse remains undefeated.

What follows depends entirely on whether this ground can truly bear what no other ground ever has.

The cross is that test.

Why Guilt Cannot Be Ignored

Before the weight can be understood, it must be named.

Guilt is not merely an emotion that can be processed, managed, or released. It is moral weight. It is the accumulated reality of choices made, harm done, and responsibility borne. It presses downward—not because a person feels badly enough, but because something real has occurred.

This is why guilt behaves differently from regret.

Regret looks backward and wishes circumstances had been different. Guilt stands in the present and insists that something must be answered for. Regret can fade with time. Guilt does not. It waits.

Every culture, regardless of its moral vocabulary, recognizes this distinction instinctively. People may deny guilt verbally, but they rarely live as though it is imaginary. They explain themselves. They justify actions. They compare themselves to others. They insist on context. These are not the behaviors of people who believe guilt is unreal. They are the behaviors of people trying to manage weight.

Psychological insight can describe guilt. Social analysis can contextualize it. Moral effort can attempt to compensate for it. But none of these can absorb it. They may soften awareness for a time, but the pressure remains. Guilt is not asking to be explained. It is asking to be resolved.

Any ground that claims to hold reality must be able to deal with guilt honestly—without denial, evasion, or collapse.

Scripture treats guilt this way. Not as a subjective feeling, but as a claim that presses for reckoning. When guilt is ignored or reframed, it does not disappear; it waits. What cannot bear it must either deny it or deflect it. Both strategies reduce pressure temporarily, but neither resolves it.

> *"If thou, LORD, shouldest mark iniquities, O Lord, who shall stand?"*
>
> *(Psalm 130:3)*
>
> *"Mine iniquities are gone over mine head: as an heavy burden they are too heavy for me."*

This is why attempts to live "beyond guilt" often fail quietly rather than dramatically. Guilt can be buried, but it cannot be neutralized. It can be hidden beneath productivity, dist-raction, or moral comparison—but it has a kind of buoyancy. Like anything pressed beneath unstable ground, it exerts upward force.

What is suppressed must be managed. What is managed requires energy. Over time, that energy cost becomes exhaustion.

This is not weakness. It is structure.

Guilt behaves this way because it is tied to reality rather than perception. Something has happened. A line has been crossed. A responsibility exists. Even if no one else knows, the ground knows. And the ground cannot forget.

This is why guilt returns unexpectedly—in moments of quiet, at times of loss, under pressure, or in the face of death. When distractions fall away and explanations thin out, what was buried presses upward again.

Sand offers one solution: delay.

On shifting ground, guilt can be reframed as misunderstanding, softened into growth, or absorbed into narrative. Responsibility becomes negotiable. The weight is not removed; it is redistributed. This feels merciful at first. But redistribution is not resolution. Over time, the accumulated pressure resurfaces—often heavier than before.

The Scriptures refuse this delay. They do not treat guilt as something to be managed indefinitely. They insist that what is real must be faced, and what is faced must be dealt with—not postponed.

This is not cruelty. It is **clarity**.

> "*Be sure your sin will find you out.*"
>
> (*Numbers 32:23*)
>
> "*Though thou wash thee with nitre, and take thee much soap, yet thine iniquity is marked before me.*"
>
> (*Jeremiah 2:22*)

If guilt could be dissolved by explanation, justice would be unnecessary. If respon-sibility could be outpaced by time, judgment would be meaningless. But the fact that guilt presses—even when denied—is evidence that reality itself is not negotiable.

Which brings us back to the test.

If the Rock is truly solid, it must be able to bear guilt without denying it, softening it, or passing it back. If it cannot, then it is no different from the sand. It may delay collapse, but it cannot prevent it.

The question is no longer whether guilt exists.

The question is where it can go.

Justice Cannot Be Set Aside

Guilt does not exist in isolation.

It carries a demand.

That demand is **justice**.

Justice is not cruelty. It is the insistence that actions matter and that wrongs are not imaginary. It is what gives moral outrage its legitimacy and forgiveness its meaning. Without justice, guilt would be little more than discomfort. With justice, guilt becomes weight.

This is why justice cannot simply be bypassed.

If guilt is real, justice must respond to it. If justice does not respond, it is no longer justice—it is sentiment. And sentiment, however compassionate it feels, cannot hold moral reality together.

This creates a dilemma that every moral system eventually faces.

If justice is enforced without mercy, the result is destruction.

If mercy is offered without justice, the result is denial.

Both outcomes fail—not emotionally, but structurally. One crushes the guilty. The other empties justice of meaning. Neither can bear the full weight of reality.

Scripture does not soften this tension. It intensifies it.

Justice is presented not as an ideal to aspire to, but as a reality that presses forward. Wrong demands judgment. Guilt demands reckoning. And when guilt is universal, the implications are severe.

If guilt were rare, justice could be selective.

If guilt were partial, justice could be measured.

But if guilt is universal—as Scripture insists—then justice, applied consistently, leads to a single outcome.

"Justice and judgment are the habitation of thy throne."

(Psalm 89:14)

"Shall not the Judge of all the earth do right?"

(Genesis 18:25)

Not correction.

Not improvement.

But judgment.

This is the point many modern moral systems quietly avoid.

They affirm justice loudly when it condemns others, but soften it instinctively when it turns inward. They demand accountability, but resist final reckoning. They want justice to matter—just not all the way down.

Sand survives by negotiation.

Justice on sand becomes adjustable. Standards are lowered. Context expands. Responsibility is redistributed. The pressure is delayed, not resolved.

This allows societies and individuals to function—but only temporarily.

The Rock does not negotiate.

If justice is real, it must be faced. If guilt is real, it must be answered. And if both are universal, then something must intervene—or destruction is inevitable.

This is not a threat.

It is a conclusion.

Universal guilt, met by uncompromising justice, cannot end in survival. The logic does not allow it. Mercy cannot be demanded at the expense of justice, and justice cannot be suspended without unraveling reality itself.

This is why the cross cannot be reduced to compassion.

It stands at the point where justice either destroys everything—or is somehow satisfied without destruction.

There is no third option.

If the Rock is truly solid, it must be able to hold justice without releasing it, and mercy without emptying it. It must bear judgment without collapsing under it, and it must do so in a way that does not deny guilt or minimize its seriousness.

That is the claim now before us.

Not that justice was ignored.

Not that guilt was softened.

But that judgment itself fell—and was held.

The Cross as Confrontation

The cross is not a religious symbol meant to inspire reflection.

It is a confrontation with reality.

At the cross, guilt is not minimized. It is exposed. Justice is not postponed. It is enacted. The question is not whether something meaningful happened, but whether the full weight we have been describing finally landed.

If guilt is real, it cannot be waved away.

If justice is real, it cannot be negotiated.

And if both are universal, then confrontation is unavoidable.

The cross is where that confrontation occurs.

Here, Scripture does not speak in metaphors or moods. It speaks in verdicts. What humanity could not carry without collapse was placed elsewhere—not ignored, not reinterpreted, but transferred. The weight did not dissolve; it fell.

This is not poetic exaggeration. It is moral relocation.

Justice did not look away.

Guilt was not excused.

Judgment did not soften.

What fell on the cross was not merely pain, but accountability. Not merely suffering, but sentence. The cross is where justice did what justice must do—without destroying those who could not survive it.

This is why the cross resists every attempt to reduce it to empathy.

Empathy can acknowledge pain.

Empathy cannot answer guilt.

Empathy can weep.

> *"The LORD hath laid on him the iniquity of us all."*
>
> *(Isaiah 53:6)*
>
> *"God hath set forth [Christ] to be a propitiation… to declare his righteousness… that he might be just, and the justifier."*
>
> *(Romans 3:25–26)*

Empathy cannot judge.

The cross is not God identifying with suffering humanity in gen-eral. It is God confronting human guilt in particular. The distinction matters. If the cross were only solidarity, justice would remain unresolved. If it were only punishment, mercy would be impossible.

> "He was wounded for our transgressions, he was bruised for our iniquities... and with his stripes we are healed."
>
> (Isaiah 53:5)
>
> "Christ also hath once suffered for sins, the just for the unjust."
>
> (1 Peter 3:18)

Scripture insists it is neither—and both.

Once.

Not repeatedly.

Not symbolically.

Not provisionally.

Once—because what was required was not improvement, but settlement.

This is the severity of the claim: the cross is where justice reached its full demand and did not go further. Nothing remained unpaid. Nothing was deferred. Nothing was left hanging over humanity waiting for later resolution.

If this is not true, then the Rock fractures here.

If justice was softened, then it was not justice.

If guilt was partially borne, then it still presses.

If the weight shifted again, then the sand remains undefeated.

But Scripture refuses those conclusions.

It presents the cross as final— not because guilt was small, but because the One bearing it was sufficient. What destroys us does not destroy Him. What fractures every other ground does not crack the Rock.

This is not reassurance.

It is declaration.

The cross is not where God asked humanity to try harder.

> *"By one offering he hath perfected for ever them that are sanctified."*
>
> *(Hebrews 10:14)*
>
> *"There is therefore now no condemnation..."*
>
> *(Romans 8:1)*

It is where God answered justice without destroying the guilty.

The confrontation has already happened.

What remains is not for guilt to be managed, or justice to be redefined, but for reality to be acknowledged. Either the weight truly fell and was held—or it did not.

And if it did not, then nothing that follows can stand.

The Weight That Fell

What fell on the cross was not confusion. It was not misunderstanding. It was not tragedy in the abstract.

> *"The LORD hath laid on him the iniquity of us all."*
>
> *(Isaiah 53:6)*
>
> *"God made him to be sin for us, who knew no sin."*
>
> *(2 Corinthians 5:21)*

It was weight.

Not symbolic weight, but moral weight—the accumulated reality of guilt, injustice, and judgment pressing toward resolution. Everything that sand cannot hold without shifting finally landed here.

Scripture does not describe the cross as a moment where weight was reduced. It describes a moment where weight was placed. What humanity carried indirectly, incompletely, and unsuccessfully was transferred—deliberately and fully.

154

This language is not therapeutic.

It is judicial.

Guilt was not treated as a feeling to be soothed, but as a reality to be borne. Justice was not relaxed, postponed, or softened. It was enacted. The weight fell because it had to fall somewhere.

And it did not fall randomly.

Scripture insists that the weight was borne willingly, not accidentally. This was not collapse under pressure, but acceptance of burden. Not victimhood, but substitution.

This matters.

If the weight fell unwillingly, the cross would be tragedy.

If it fell unknowingly, the cross would be injustice.

If it fell partially, the cross would be insufficient.

But Scripture refuses all three.

What fell was known.

> *"I lay down my life... No man taketh it from me."*
>
> *(John 10:17–18)*
>
> *"Who for the joy that was set before him endured the cross."*
>
> *(Hebrews 12:2)*

What fell was chosen.

What fell was complete.

This is why the cross cannot be reduced to an example of sac-rifice. Examples invite imitation. The cross invites no such thing. No one is asked to carry this weight again. It was carried once because it could only be carried once.

> *"He shall bear their iniquities."*
>
> *(Isaiah 53:11)*
>
> *"When he had by himself purged our sins…"*
>
> *(Hebrews 1:3)*

The pressure that fractures every other ground did not fracture here. The burden that crushes human systems did not overwhelm the Rock. What falls on sand disperses and sinks. What fell on the Rock was received and held.

Nothing in this account suggests mitigation.

Nothing suggests delay.

Nothing suggests remainder.

The weight did not shift again.

If guilt still presses, it does not press because it was left unresolved.

If justice still matters, it does not matter because it was ignored.

If judgment was required, it was not avoided.

It fell.

And what fell did not return.

This is not comfort yet.

It is finality.

The question now is not whether the weight was real.

The question is whether the Rock held.

Why the Rock Does Not Break

The question is unavoidable.

Every other ground fractures under this weight. Guilt overwhelms. Justice destroys. Death ends the argument. If the Rock truly bore what no other ground can bear, then something fundamentally different must be true of it.

Scripture does not answer this by appealing to endurance alone. The Rock does not hold because it tries harder, absorbs more pain, or endures longer. It holds because it is not subject to the same limitations as the ground that fails.

The weight did not break the Rock because the Rock is not part of the system that produced the weight.

Guilt presses because responsibility exists between creatures. Justice destroys because finite beings cannot survive full reckoning. Death reigns because everything that begins must end. These forces dominate every human structure because every human structure shares the same condition: limitation.

The Rock does not.

> *"Before the mountains were brought forth... even from everlasting to everlasting, thou art God."*
>
> *(Psalm 90:2)*
>
> *"In him we live, and move, and have our being."*
>
> *(Acts 17:28)*

Scripture presents Christ not merely as a better human response to guilt, but as ground of a different order altogether. Not created, not contingent, not dependent. The One who bore the weight is not sustained by the ground beneath Him—He is the ground.

This is why judgment does not overwhelm Him.

Justice consumes what it finds guilty. It does not consume righteousness. The weight of judgment destroys those who must answer for their own guilt. It does not destroy the One in whom no guilt exists.

Scripture is explicit here—not defensively, but plainly.

What would crush us does not crush Him because it is not His guilt being judged. The weight He bears is not the exposure of His failure, but the reckoning of ours.

And this is where substitution ceases to be theory and becomes necessity.

If the One bearing the weight were guilty, justice would destroy Him.

> *"Which of you convinceth me of sin?"*
>
> *(John 8:46)*
>
> *"He knew no sin."*
>
> *(2 Corinthians 5:21)*

> *"Thou art my Son; this day have I begotten thee."*
>
> *(Psalm 2:7)*
>
> *"All things were made by him; and without him was not any thing made that was made."*
>
> *(John 1:3)*

If He were merely human, the burden would exceed His capacity.

If He were distant from judgment, the weight would remain unresolved.

But Scripture presents something else entirely.

The Rock holds because it is not upheld by anything else. It does not depend on justice being lenient or guilt being small. It stands beneath justice and above guilt. The weight falls onto it because there is nowhere else for it to go.

This is not strength in the ordinary sense.

It is category difference.

The Rock does not survive judgment by evasion.

It does not endure justice by negotiation.

It does not overcome death by resistance.

It holds because it cannot be undone.

> *"I am the LORD, I change not."*
>
> *(Malachi 3:6)*
>
> *"Jesus Christ the same yesterday, and to day, and for ever."*
>
> *(Hebrews 13:8)*

This is why the weight does not fracture the Rock.

Not because judgment was light.

Not because guilt was softened.

But because the One bearing it stands outside the conditions that make collapse inevitable.

Every other ground gives way because it must.

This one does not—because it cannot.

And that leaves only one question unanswered.

If the weight truly fell here, and if the Rock truly did not break, then the final test is not guilt or justice, but death itself.

What This Means for the Pit

The pit has not disappeared.

People still fall into it. Guilt still accumulates. Justice still presses. Death still looms.

What has changed is not the presence of the pit, but its authority.

Before the weight fell on the Rock, the pit functioned as final ground. Once a person sank far enough, there was nowhere else to stand. Collapse was not just likely; it was inevitable. The pit was not merely a condition—it was a verdict.

The cross changes that.

Scripture presents the pit as real —but no longer sovereign.

> *"He brought me up also out of an horrible pit, out of the miry clay, and set my feet upon a rock."*
>
> *(Psalm 40:2)*

It does not deny the pit's reality, but it exposes its limits. The pit no longer defines what is ultimate. It is no longer the deepest place weight can go.

This is not escape by effort.

It is interruption by strength.

The pit is where weight accumulates when it has nowhere else to land. Guilt presses downward. Justice closes in. Explanations thin. Language fails. The walls narrow. Eventually, the person stops asking why and begins asking how long.

But the cross introduces a deeper ground beneath the pit itself.

What once collected there—unanswered guilt, unresolved justice, unescapable judgment—has been met elsewhere. The pit is no longer the place where weight must finally settle. It has been undercut.

This does not mean the pit feels shallow.

It means it is no longer decisive.

Scripture describes this shift carefully. It does not say the pit was filled in. It says a way out was established —one that does not originate from within the pit and cannot be climbed by effort.

The pit still tells a story: You are stuck. You are buried. This is where it ends.

But that story is no longer true.

The cross confronts the pit at its deepest claim—that guilt and justice inevitably end in dest-ruction—and contradicts it. The pit can accuse. It cannot condemn. It can press. It cannot decide.

This is why despair is no longer honest.

Not because circumstances improve.

Not because weight feels lighter.

But because the pit has been exposed as secondary ground.

The weight that once made the pit final has already fallen elsewhere.

And because of that, relocation is now conceivable.

Not yet explained.

Not yet offered.

But no longer impossible.

The pit remains—but it no longer owns the bottom.

> *"For thou wilt not leave my soul in hell; neither wilt thou suffer thine Holy One to see corruption."*
>
> *(Psalm 16:10)*
>
> *"I am he that liveth, and was dead; and, behold, I am alive for evermore... and have the keys of hell and of death."*
>
> *(Revelation 1:18)*

Not an Invitation Yet, but a Declaration

This chapter is not asking for a response. It is making a claim about reality.

Either the cross is where the full weight of guilt and justice was borne—or it is not. There is no middle ground between those two statements, and no way to soften their implications.

If the weight did not truly fall, then the Rock is no different from the sand. It may delay collapse, but it cannot prevent it. The pit remains undefeated, and everything described in the earlier chapters still stands.

But if the weight did fall—if guilt was borne without denial and justice was satisfied without destruction—then the structure of reality itself has changed.

Not emotionally.

Not symbolically.

Structurally.

Scripture does not present the cross as an offer awaiting acceptance, but as an event that has already occurred. Something was done before anyone responded to it. Something was settled before anyone stood upon it.

Finished does not mean explained. It does not mean applied. It means *completed*.

What required judgment has been judged. What required bearing has been borne. What demanded settlement has been settled.

This declaration does not yet tell anyone where to stand. It tells them where standing has become possible.

The pit has not vanished, but it has been exposed as secondary ground. Sand still shifts, guilt still presses, justice still matters—but none of them are final anymore. The deepest weight has already landed, and it did not fracture the Rock.

This is not reassurance. It is relocation made conceivable.

Before response comes recognition.

Before movement comes ground.

> *"When Jesus therefore had received the vinegar, he said, It is finished: and he bowed his head, and gave up the ghost."*
>
> *(John 19:30)*
>
> *"After he had offered one sacrifice for sins for ever, sat down on the right hand of God."*
>
> *(Hebrews 10:12)*

The only question left open by this chapter is not what should be done, but what actually happened.

Did the Rock hold?

If it did not, then the cross was collapse, not resolution. If it did, then standing is no longer imaginary.

Everything now depends on whether the Rock broke —or whether it remained.

That question cannot be answered by reflection or feeling.

It can only be answered by what happened next.

Summary

This chapter has presented the cross as the decisive test of whether the Rock can bear the weight of reality. Guilt cannot be ignored, and justice cannot be bypassed. Any foundation that claims to hold must be able to absorb both without collapse.

The claim of the Christian faith is that the weight humanity cannot carry was placed on the Rock and fully borne. The cross is not an explanation of suffering, but the resolution of guilt and justice together.

If this claim is true, then the instability described in Part I is no longer final.

Application: Questions of Ground

1. Why does guilt feel heavier than regret or mistake?

2. What would justice require if wrongs are truly real?

3. Can forgiveness have meaning without justice? Why or why not?

4. If moral weight must be borne rather than ignored, where could it possibly go?

5. What would it mean if the cross is not symbolic, but structural?

6. If the weight has been carried, what might that make possible?

Where to Stand

7

The Ground That Did Not Crack

The Question That Cannot Be Avoided

If the weight truly fell on the Rock, there is only one question left to ask.

Did it hold?

Everything depends on this. Not because the cross lacked severity, but because severity alone does not prove endurance. Many things absorb pressure briefly. Many structures survive a moment of strain. What matters is not whether the Rock was tested, but whether it fractured under the test that breaks everything else.

Death is that test.

Death is not merely the end of biological function. It is the final pressure reality applies. It is the point where guilt, justice, and judgment converge. No explanation survives it. No system absorbs it. Every human structure eventually yields to it.

If the Rock cracked here, then the cross was not resolution—it was collapse. If death held Him, then guilt was not exhausted, justice was not satisfied, and the pit remains undefeated. The weight would still be pressing, merely displaced for a moment.

But if death did not hold Him—if the Rock remained— then the verdict rendered at the cross was not provisional. It was final.

This is why the resurrection is not an afterthought. It is not a hopeful addendum to the crucifixion. It is the only possible answer to the question Chapter 6 leaves open.

Scripture presents the resurrection this way—not as encouragement, but as consequence. Not as a belief to be adopted, but as a fact that either stands or collapses under scrutiny.

Notice what is being claimed.

If the Rock broke, guilt remains.

If death held Him, justice was not resolved.

If the tomb stayed sealed, the ground beneath reality is still sand.

Scripture does not ask the reader to feel reassured about these things. It asks them to be honest about what follows if the resurrection did not occur. There is no middle position where the cross "mostly worked" but death still wins. Either the ground held —or it did not.

And this is why the resurrection cannot be reduced to metaphor.

Metaphors do not empty tombs. Symbols do not reverse death. Hope does not shatter finality.

Only endurance does.

The question before us, then, is not whether resurrection is comforting, meaningful, or inspiring. The question is whether the Rock remained intact when the full weight of death pressed down upon it.

If it did not, nothing that follows can stand.

> "Whom God hath raised up, having loosed the pains of death: because it was not possible that he should be holden of it."
>
> (Acts 2:24)

> "If Christ be not raised, your faith is vain; ye are yet in your sins."
>
> (1 Corinthians 15:17)

If it did, then the ground beneath everything has changed—and the change is irreversible.

That question cannot be avoided.

Everything now turns on the answer.

Death as the Final Test

Death applies the pressure nothing else can.

Every system eventually encounters it. Every explanation weakens before it. Every attempt to reinterpret reality runs out of language here. Death does not negotiate. It does not wait for meaning to catch up. It ends arguments by force.

This is why death exposes foundations.

As long as death can be postponed, systems can function. As long as it can be ignored, weight can be redistributed. But when death arrives, every substitute ground is tested at once. Guilt can no longer be reframed. Justice can no longer be deferred. Consequences are no longer theoretical.

Death is where sand always gives way.

This is not because death is dramatic, but because it is final. It is the point where all moral accounting comes due. Whatever remains unresolved before death is resolved by it—or destroyed by it.

Scripture consistently treats death this way. Not merely as biological failure, but as the culmination of moral rupture. It is the last expression of guilt and judgment pressing toward completion.

Because death is final, survival here proves something no other survival can.

If a system collapses under suffering but survives death, it has not survived at all. If a structure absorbs injustice but yields to death, it was never solid. Endurance that ends at death is endurance only in appearance.

> *"The wages of sin is death."*
>
> *(Romans 6:23)*
>
> *"It is appointed unto men once to die, but after this the judgment."*
>
> *(Hebrews 9:27)*

This is why the resurrection matters—not as hope beyond death, but as verdict over it.

If death held Him, then the cross did not settle what it claimed to settle. Judgment would still stand. Guilt would still press. The pit would remain undefeated. The Rock would have fractured at the point where every other ground fractures.

But if death did not hold Him, then the test has been passed at the deepest possible level.

Scripture states this plainly—not as reflection, but as fact.

"Not possible" is a severe phrase.

It does not mean unlikely.

It does not mean surprising.

It means death lacked authority.

> *"God raised him from the dead, loosing the pains of d e a t h : because it was not possible that he should be holden of it."*
>
> *(Acts 2:24)*

The resurrection is not about returning from danger. It is about death being exhausted of its claim. What was applied fully did not prevail. What pressed with finality did not win.

Death did what it always does. And for the first time, it failed.

That failure is not inspirational.

It is diagnostic.

It tells us something about the ground beneath reality —something no philosophy, system, or moral effort has ever demonstrated. It tells us that the weight that produces death was already dealt with before death arrived.

Which means death was not the final word.

The question now is not whether this matters, but what kind of event could produce such a result.

Because death does not release what it still owns.

The Silence of the Tomb

What Scripture describes is not a return to life as it was before.

Resuscitation happens within the same system. It restores what was failing, but it does not change the conditions that caused the failure. A resuscitated life remains subject to decay, judgment, and death. The pressure returns because the ground has not changed.

That is not what is being claimed here.

If the resurrection were merely resuscitation, then death would still hold authority. It would have released Him temporarily, only to reclaim Him later. The Rock would not have passed the test—it would have delayed the outcome.

Scripture refuses that interpretation.

The resurrection is presented not as recovery, but as exit. Not as survival within death's jurisdiction, but as the breaking of its claim. What rose did not rise back into the old order. It rose out of it.

These are not poetic flourishes. They are categorical statements.

> *"Christ being raised from the dead dieth no more; death hath no more dominion over him."*
>
> *(Romans 6:9)*
>
> *"I am he that liveth, and was dead; and, behold, I am alive for evermore."*

Death no longer exercises authority. Judgment no longer presses. Decay no longer advances.

If resurrection were resuscitation, none of this could be said.

Resuscitation leaves the weight in place. Resurrection proves the weight has been exhausted. The difference is not duration, but jurisdiction.

Scripture reinforces this distinction by describing what rose as transformed, not merely restored. The body that emerges is continuous with what died—but no longer governed by the same limits.

> *"It is sown in corruption; it is raised in incorruption... it is sown a natural body; it is raised a spiritual body."*
>
> *(1 Corinthians 15:42–44)*

This matters for the argument of the book.

If the resurrection were simply a reversal of death, then the Rock would still be standing inside the same unstable ground. Death would remain undefeated. The pit would still be final—it would simply take longer.

But if the resurrection marks the end of death's authority, then something decisive has occurred. The test has not merely been survived; it has been passed.

Death applied its full pressure. The Rock did not crack. And what emerged was not subject to death again.

That is not continuation.

That is **confirmation**.

The resurrection confirms that the weight that produces death has already been dealt with. Justice has been satisfied. Guilt has been exhausted. Judgment has reached its limit and gone no further.

Which means the ground beneath reality is no longer provisional.

What remains to be shown is how this was made known, and why the claim did not remain private, symbolic, or hidden.

Because a ground that truly holds does not stay buried.

When the Ground Held

The resurrection declares something unmistakable: the Rock did not break.

Death applied its full pressure—and failed. The force that fractures every other foundation pressed down here without producing collapse. What had crushed every human structure met a ground that remained intact.

> *"Behold my hands and my feet, that it is I myself: handle me, and see; for a spirit hath not flesh and bones, as ye see me have."*
>
> *(Luke 24:39)*

> *"Jesus saith unto her, Mary. She turned herself, and saith unto him, Rabboni."*
>
> *(John 20:16)*

This is not presented as metaphor.

Scripture insists on physicality, presence, and continuity. What rose was not an idea, not a memory, not a spiritual impression. The same One who bore the weight stood again—recognizable, identifiable, continuous in identity, yet no longer subject to the conditions that had killed Him.

This matters because collapse would have erased continuity.

178

If the Rock had fractured, nothing recognizable would have remained. Identity would have dissolved. Presence would have been impossible. What survives death only as memory or symbol has not survived at all.

But Scripture presents something else.

The One who bore judgment was not replaced. The One who entered death was not lost. The One who fell under the weight stood again.

The ground held.

> "I am he that liveth, and was dead; and, behold, I am alive for evermore."
>
> (Revelation 1:18)

What rose was not returned to the old order, but neither was it disconnected from what died. The weight-bearing foundation did not give way, and because it did not, what stood afterward was not a substitute — but the same ground, now proven.

This is not reassurance yet. It is verification. The test was applied. The pressure was complete. The foundation remained.

The Rock did not break.

What the Resurrection Verifies

The resurrection does not add meaning to the cross; it verifies it.

It confirms that the weight was fully borne, not partially managed. That justice was satisfied, not postponed. That guilt was resolved, not displaced. That the pit has no ultimate claim.

If the cross were incomplete, death would have remained. If guilt were unresolved, the ground would have cracked. Nothing short of collapse would have followed.

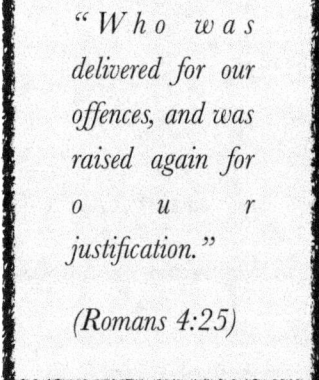

" Who was delivered for our offences, and was raised again for o u r justification."

(Romans 4:25)

The empty tomb is not only a symbol of hope. It is evidence of completion.

This is why the resurrection is not optional to the Christian claim. Without it, the Rock would be no different from sand—capable of absorbing pressure briefly, but unable to hold when the final weight fell.

A New Plane of Standing

Something else becomes visible here—something subtle, but decisive.

Where to Stand

The resurrection does not simply return Jesus to life within the old order. It introduces a new plane of reality. What stands afterward does not stand where everything else stands. The Rock is revealed not only as stable, but as generative. Life now flows from what bore death.

This is not recovery. It is emergence.

Scripture consistently describes what followed the resurrection as new in kind, not merely renewed in condition. What rose did not re-enter the system that produced collapse. It stood beyond it. The ground that held under judgment now becomes the ground from which life proceeds.

> *"Christ is risen from the dead, and become the firstfruits of them that slept."*
>
> *(1 Corinthians 15:20)*

Firstfruits do not stand alone. They indicate what kind of ground now exists. They mark the beginning of a harvest, not the exception to it. What appears here is not an isolated victory, but the unveiling of a different order of standing.

This is the first glimpse of relocation—not yet explained, not yet applied, but now possible.

Standing is no longer imagined. It has occurred.

The question is no longer whether such ground exists. The question is how anyone who remains on sand could come to stand there.

Why This Changes Everything

If the Rock held under death, then nothing else can dislodge those who stand upon it.

Death is the final pressure reality applies. What remains after it is not provisional. If the foundation did not give way here, then no lesser force can undo it. Instability is no longer ultimate. Justice has been satisfied. Guilt has been carried. Death has been defeated—not ignored, not bypassed, but passed through and exhausted.

> *"He that heareth my words, and believeth on him that sent me, hath everlasting life, and shall not come into condemnation; but is passed from death unto life."*

Scripture speaks of this change in terms of permanence rather than feeling. What has been established is not fragile. It is not maintained by effort or sustained by circumstance. It stands because the ground itself holds.

This does not eliminate suffering. It does not remove responsibility. It does not insulate life from pressure.

182

But it changes the ground on which all of it is faced.

What once threatened collapse can no longer determine outcome. What once pressed toward judgment has already reached its limit. The weight that destabilized everything else has been borne where it could do no further damage.

Reality is no longer a shifting surface.

It has a foundation.

Not Yet the Invitation

Once again, this chapter does not ask for response. It declares what has happened.

The Rock was tested.

The weight was applied.

The ground did not crack.

These are not personal conclusions. They are claims about reality itself. They stand whether they are welcomed or resisted. Nothing here depends on agreement or reaction.

Only now does it make sense to speak of being placed on that ground.

Before placement, there had to be proof. Before invitation, there had to be endurance. Before standing could be offered, the ground itself had to hold.

That question has now been answered.

What follows is not persuasion, but explanation. Not pressure, but clarity. Not demand, but disclosure.

Standing is no longer hypothetical. It is possible—because the ground is real.

Summary

This chapter applies the final test.

If the Rock truly bore the weight described in the previous chapter, then it had to withstand the one force that fractures every other foundation. That force is death. Death is not symbolic pressure or emotional crisis; it is the final boundary. Whatever cannot hold here does not hold at all.

The resurrection answers this test.

It declares that the Rock did not break. Death pressed down with its full force and failed to fracture the foundation. What rose was not a replacement, a memory, or a spiritual impression, but the same One who bore the weight—continuous in identity, transformed in condition, no longer subject to death's authority.

This matters because collapse would have erased continuity. Survival only as symbol or sentiment would have proven failure. But Scripture presents something else: endurance, presence, and permanence.

The resurrection does not add meaning to the cross; it verifies it. It confirms that the weight was fully borne, justice was satisfied, guilt was resolved, and the pit no longer holds ultimate claim. The empty tomb is not an emblem of hope; it is evidence of completion.

What emerges is not a return to the old order, but the unveiling of a new plane of standing. Life now flows from what bore death. The ground that held under judgment is revealed as generative, not merely stable.

Because the Rock held under death, nothing lesser can dislodge those who stand upon it. Instability is no longer ultimate. Suffering remains real. Responsibility remains intact. But the ground on which both are faced has changed. Reality is no longer a shifting surface. It has a foundation.

This chapter does not ask for response. It declares what has happened. The Rock was tested. The weight was applied. The ground did not crack.

Now we can ask whether anyone can stand upon it.

Application: Questions of Ground

1. Why must the resurrection be more than encouragement to matter?

2. What would it mean if death is not the final pressure reality applies?

3. How does the resurrection change the meaning of justice and guilt?

4. If the ground held under death, what could possibly destabilize it?

5. What would it mean for standing to be given rather than achieved?

6. If relocation is possible, what might still stand in the way?

III

Standing Where Life Can Grow

Where to Stand

8

Placed on Solid Ground

When Standing Becomes Possible

Up to this point, the question has been whether solid ground exists and whether it can bear weight. That question has now been answered. The Rock has been revealed, tested, and proven. It did not crack under guilt, justice, or death.

Only now does a new question come into view—one that could not have been asked earlier.

How does anyone come to stand on that ground?

This question could not be raised while the ground itself was uncertain. It would have been meaningless to speak of standing where no stable place existed. But once the Rock is shown to hold, the problem shifts from existence to placement.

The answer must be consistent with everything already established.

If standing could be achieved by effort, we would be back in the miry pit—measuring progress, negotiating standards, and redistributing weight that cannot be carried. If standing depended on improvement, sincerity, or moral strength, the ground would shift again. What is earned can be lost. What is achieved must be maintained. What depends on performance is always provisional.

Whatever standing is, it cannot arise from within the pit.

It must not depend on climbing, striving, or deserving. It must not require the weight to be carried again. It must not ask the unstable to stabilize themselves.

If standing is real, it must be given.

Not as reward.

Not as recognition.

But as relocation.

Only a ground that has already held can bear someone being placed upon it. And only placement—received rather than achieved—can explain how anyone who could not hold the weight could now stand where the weight has already been borne.

Standing becomes possible not because people finally become strong enough to stand, but because the ground beneath them is.

Standing Is a Matter of Placement

Standing is not a feeling. It is not confidence. It is not resolve.

Standing is **location**.

To stand is to be placed where weight can be borne. To be unable to stand is not primarily a failure of will, but of ground. The difference between sinking and standing is not strength, but position.

This is why the language of relocation matters.

The Christian claim is not that people are strengthened enough to stand where they are. It is that they are moved—set down on ground that already holds. What could not be borne before is not suddenly made lighter. It has already been carried. Standing does not begin with effort; it begins with placement.

Scripture consistently speaks of this change not as self-improvement, but as a change of standing before God. What was unstable is replaced. What could not

> *"Therefore being justified by faith, we have peace with God through our Lord Jesus Christ:*
>
> *By whom also we have access by faith into this grace wherein we stand."*
>
> *(Romans 5:1–2)*

bear weight is exchanged for what can.

Notice what changes here.

Nothing in the person's past is revised. The weight already borne does not need to be reprocessed. The record is not renegotiated. The change is not internal first. It is positional.

Standing occurs because a verdict has already been rendered and a place has already been prepared. What follows in a person's life will matter—but it cannot be the cause of standing. It can only be the result.

Standing is not achieved from below. It is received from above.

Why This Is Not Moral Improvement

This point must be made carefully, because it is easily misunderstood.

Relocation does not mean that behavior immediately improves or that moral struggle disappears. It means that moral struggle is no longer taking place on collapsing ground. The difference is not the absence of pressure, but the presence of stability.

Improvement belongs to growth.

Standing belongs to **placement**.

When these are confused, everything unravels.

> *"...this grace wherein we stand."*
>
> *(Romans 5:2)*

If standing is treated as the result of improvement, then effort becomes the condition of stability. Faith quietly turns into performance. Obedience becomes leverage. Progress is measured as proof of belonging. And the ground begins to shift again—this time under religious language.

The pit returns, but with better vocabulary.

This confusion is especially dangerous because it sounds serious and sincere. It produces striving that feels virtuous and failure that feels condemning. But it reverses the order of reality. It asks growth to do the work that only placement can do.

Standing on solid ground does not follow moral progress. It precedes it.

Growth that comes after standing is real growth. Struggle that occurs on solid ground is honest struggle. Responsibility does not vanish—but it is no longer carrying the weight of justification.

What changes is not the existence of effort, but what effort is for.

Standing answers the question of **where**.

Growth answers the question of **how**.

Confusing the two does not produce holiness.

It produces instability—again.

A New Relation to Judgment

Once a person is placed on solid ground, judgment is no longer a threat—it has already been faced and resolved. The ground beneath them has absorbed the weight they could not bear.

This does not eliminate accountability. It repositions it.

Instead of standing before judgment on unstable ground, the person now stands after judgment on ground that has already held. Justice has been satisfied, not suspended. Guilt has been resolved, not denied. What once pressed toward condemnation has already reached its limit and gone no further.

Scripture speaks of this shift not as exemption, but as **passage**. Judgment is not avoided; it is passed through. What changes is not the seriousness of justice, but the location from which it is faced.

This is why assurance is possible. Not because the person is strong. Not because failure has become impossible. But because judgment has already been borne where it could do no further damage.

The ground beneath them has been tested by justice itself— and did not crack.

> *"He that heareth my words, and believeth on him that sent me, hath everlasting life, and shall not come into condemnation; but is passed from death unto life."*
>
> *(John 5:24)*

What Faith Actually Is

At this point, the word faith must be clarified.

Faith is not belief that something might be true.

It is not optimism.

It is not resolve to live differently.

Faith is **reliance**.

It is the end of the struggle to stand and the acceptance of being placed. It does not create the ground. It does not strengthen it. It does not test it. It rests on it.

Faith does not move a person onto solid ground. It acknowledges that they have been moved. It is the recognition that standing is now possible because something outside the self has already been done.

This is why faith cannot be measured by intensity or consistency. Its value does not lie in itself, but in what it rests upon. A trembling foot on solid ground stands more securely than confident strides on sand.

Scripture describes faith in these terms—not as exertion, but as rest. Not as effort applied upward, but as weight set down.

> *"For he that is entered into his rest, he also hath ceased from his own works."*
>
> *(Hebrews 4:10)*

Faith does not compete with obedience, but it precedes it. It does not replace responsibility, but it removes responsibility from the work of standing. What follows faith will matter—but it cannot be the cause of placement. It can only be the result of it.

Faith is not the mechanism that saves. It is the posture that recognizes salvation has already occurred.

Standing does not begin when faith becomes strong.

Faith begins when standing is no longer in question.

Standing Without Earning

One of the hardest things to accept is that standing does not need to be maintained by effort.

The instinct to earn does not disappear easily. Even after being placed on solid ground, many continue trying to justify their place—measuring worth, proving sincerity, and watching for signs that the ground might give way. Old habits of survival persist long after survival is no longer required.

But solid ground does not require constant proving.

It holds whether the one standing feels strong or weak. It bears weight regardless of confidence. Stability does not fluctuate with emotion, performance, or awareness. The security of the ground does not depend on the steadiness of the one standing upon it.

> *"Who are kept by the power of God through faith."*
>
> *(1 Peter 1:5)*

Scripture speaks of this security not as something fragile that must be preserved, but as something upheld from beneath.

This is what makes growth possible.

197

As long as effort is spent trying to remain justified, it cannot be spent living faithfully. As long as standing feels conditional, obedience remains defensive. But when standing is secure, effort is freed from survival and redirected toward life.

Growth does not establish standing.

Standing makes growth possible.

Effort no longer answers the question of whether one belongs.

It begins to answer the question of how one lives— now that belonging is settled.

Life Can Now Take Root

Ground that holds allows soil to settle.

Where collapse is no longer constant, roots can form. Growth can occur without panic. Life no longer has to be spent bracing against failure; it can begin to move outward and upward.

This marks the transition from justification to transformation—not as a shift in strategy, but as a consequence of standing. Nothing new is required. Nothing additional is earned. What changes is not the goal, but the condition under which growth takes place.

Where to Stand

When standing is secure, growth is no longer frantic.

When standing is settled, obedience is no longer leverage. Life begins to grow upward because it is anchored downward.

Scripture consistently presents growth this way—not as the means of stability, but as its fruit.

Roots do not form in shifting ground. They require stability beneath the surface. In the same way, transformation does not begin with effort applied upward, but with weight already borne below.

> *"And being rooted and built up in h i m, a n d stablished..."*
>
> *(Colossians 2:7)*

This is what relocation makes possible.

When the ground beneath life is stable, growth no longer has to justify existence. Roots can deepen without fear of collapse. Obedience can proceed without anxiety. Life begins to unfold from security rather than strain.

Growth no longer exists to preserve standing.

Standing has already been secured.

Summary

This chapter has described what it means to stand on solid ground. Standing is not achieved through effort or improvement, but given through relocation. It is a change of position, not performance.

Faith is not a new form of struggle, but reliance on ground that already holds. Because judgment has been resolved and guilt borne, assurance becomes possible—not because the person is strong, but because the foundation is secure.

Only on this ground can life truly grow.

Application: Questions of Ground

1. How do you typically measure whether you are "doing well"?

2. Have you ever treated improvement as proof that you belong on solid ground?

3. What would change if standing were secure before growth began?

4. How does reliance differ from effort in your own thinking?

5. What fears surface when the idea of unearned standing is presented?

6. If you were truly placed on solid ground, where might growth naturally follow?

Where to Stand

9

Stepping Off the Sand

When Response Finally Makes Sense

Only after solid ground has been revealed, tested, and shown to hold does response become meaningful.

Before this point, calls to faith and repentance would have sounded like another demand for effort— another attempt to climb out of the pit by resolve, sincerity, or reform. They would have asked the unstable to stabilize themselves, the sinking to generate footing where none existed.

But now the situation has changed.

Standing is possible. The ground beneath reality is firm. Relocation has occurred.

Because of this, the question itself has shifted. It is no longer how does one save oneself? That question has already been answered—and removed. The question now is how life is to be lived in alignment with what is already true.

Response no longer functions as rescue.

It becomes **recognition**.

This is where faith and repentance belong—not as mechanisms for gaining ground, but as the human response to ground that has already been given. They are not the means by which standing is achieved, but the way a person begins to live once standing is real.

Only now does response make sense.

Faith as Visibility

Faith is often misunderstood as belief strong enough to produce results. In practice, this turns faith into a form of effort—a psychological substitute for moral resolve. When faith is treated this way, it becomes fragile and exhausting, because it is asked to do work it was never meant to do.

But faith, properly understood, does not create reality.

It brings reality into view.

Faith is the visible alignment of life with what has already been established. It does not make the Rock solid. It recognizes that the Rock is solid. It does not produce standing. It lives in light of the fact that standing has already been given.

In this sense, faith is not primarily internal. It is observable. It shows itself in the way life is oriented once the ground beneath it is no longer in question. Faith looks like living as though the truth is actually true.

> *"For we walk by faith, not by sight."*
>
> *(2 Corinthians 5:7)*

This is why faith cannot be measured by intensity, certainty, or emotion. Those fluctuate. Faith is measured by coherence. It is the consistency between what is real and how life is ordered in response to it.

Faith looks like living as though Christ is actually Lord — **because He is.**

Confession as Alignment, Not Incantation

This understanding clarifies the meaning of confession.

Scripture speaks of confessing Jesus as Lord—not as a ritual phrase meant to trigger salvation, and not as a verbal mechanism that produces standing, but as an act of alignment. Confession is the point at which what is known to be true is no longer held at a distance. It is allowed to shape how life is actually lived.

> *"If thou shalt confess with thy mouth the Lord Jesus, and shalt believe in thine heart that God hath raised him from the dead, thou shalt be saved."*
>
> *(Romans 10:9)*

To confess Christ as Lord is to stop behaving as though authority is still negotiable. It is to abandon the pretense that one stands on self-chosen ground. Confession does not establish reality; it acknowledges it. It makes visible where a person is already standing.

In this sense, confession is not performative. It is **revelatory**.

Scripture describes confession this way—not as incantation, but as agreement with what is already the case.

Notice the order implied here. Confession does not summon authority; it submits to it. It does not create lordship; it names it. What is spoken outwardly corresponds to what has already been acknowledged inwardly and established objectively.

This is why confession cannot earn standing. Standing has already been given. The ground has already held.

Confession simply stops pretending otherwise.

It is the moment when alignment replaces negotiation —when life begins to cohere publicly with what is now undeniably true.

Belief That Reality Has Shifted

Faith also involves belief—but not merely agreement with ideas.

To believe that God raised Jesus from the dead is not simply to accept a claim. It is to accept that the Rock held under death and that reality itself has

> *"If thou shalt believe in thine heart that God hath raised him from the dead, thou shalt be saved."*
>
> *(Romans 10:9)*

been reordered. The resurrection is not an isolated miracle added to an otherwise unchanged world. It is the confirmation that guilt has been resolved, judgment has been faced, and instability is no longer ultimate.

Belief, then, is not passive assent.

It is the acceptance of a new reality—and the refusal to continue living as though the old one still governs. To believe is to acknowledge that the decisive event has already occurred and that life must now be oriented accordingly.

Scripture consistently presents belief this way—not as mental agreement detached from life, but as acknowledgment of what God has actually done in history.

Notice what belief is directed toward here. It is not belief in personal potential, moral improvement, or religious effort. It is belief in a completed act—an event that has already reshaped the ground beneath reality.

> *"God hath made that same Jesus... both Lord and Christ."*
>
> *(Acts 2:36)*

This is why belief without visible alignment feels hollow.

Not because belief must prove itself, and not because alignment earns standing, but because belief that remains abstract has not yet been allowed to take full account of what is now true. When reality shifts, belief that recognizes the shift inevitably begins to reshape how life is lived.

Belief does not manufacture reality.

It responds to it.

Repentance as Directional Change

Repentance has suffered from similar mis-understanding.

It is often reduced to remorse or self-reproach—an inward spiral of regret that traps people in introspection rather than movement. But repentance is not self-condemnation. It is reorientation.

Repentance means turning off the sand—not because sand is unpleasant, but because it cannot hold. It is the practical outworking of relocation. Repentance does not create standing; it is the movement that follows once standing has been acknowledged. Having been placed on solid ground, the person now begins to move consistently with that ground.

> "*That they should repent and turn to God, and do works meet for repentance.*"
>
> *(Acts 26:20)*

This change is not primarily emotional.

It is **directional**.

Repentance does not ask a person to replay the past endlessly. It asks them to stop walking as though the old ground still governs the present. What has already been judged no longer needs to be re-judged. What has already failed no longer needs to be tested again.

Scripture speaks of repentance in these terms—not as inward anguish, but as a visible turning that follows recognition of what is true.

Notice the order. Turning precedes fruit. Direction changes before life reshapes. Repentance does not earn new ground; it begins to walk in accordance with it.

This is why repentance is not immediate perfection. It is coherence over time.

Life begins to align, step by step, with the reality that now supports it. Movement replaces paralysis. Direction replaces fixation. What once pulled inward now moves outward—away from collapse and toward what can actually hold.

Repentance is not an attempt to feel differently. It is the decision to **live** differently because reality is different.

Why Faith and Repentance Are Not Works

At this point, an objection often arises: if faith and repentance involve visible change, aren't they simply another form of works?

The answer is no—because they are not attempts to achieve standing. They are the consequence of having been given standing.

Works attempt to build ground. Faith and repentance assume ground already exists. The difference is decisive.

Works are efforts to establish stability where none exists. They aim upward, trying to construct what can bear weight. Faith and repentance move in the opposite direction. They begin with recognition. They respond to what has already been established and proven to hold.

> "For we are his workmanship, created in Christ Jesus unto good works, which God hath before ordained that we should walk in them."
>
> (Ephesians 2:10)

A person standing on solid ground does not need to prove it by effort. They do not reinforce the foundation by exertion. They simply live in a way that makes sense given where they are standing.

Scripture draws this same distinction—not by opposing action, but by ordering it correctly.

Notice the sequence. The work is prepared before the walking begins. Action follows placement; it does not create it. What is lived out is not a bid for standing, but the natural expression of it.

This is why faith and repentance cannot be leveraged.

They do not earn ground. They do not secure belonging. They do not stabilize what is unstable.

They make visible what is already true.

Faith acknowledges the ground that holds. Repentance adjusts direction to match it.

Neither builds the foundation. Both acknowledge it.

Leaving the Pit Behind

"And be not conformed to this world: but be ye transformed by the renewing of your mind."

(Romans 12:2)

One of the most difficult transitions is letting go of the pit's logic.

Even after relocation, many continue to think as though standing must be maintained by effort. Old habits linger. Old currencies reassert themselves. Old measurements and fears quietly return. Life is still interpreted through the instincts formed on collapsing ground.

But the pit has no authority once the ground has changed.

The danger is not that a person will fall back into the pit by accident, but that they will continue to live as though it still governs reality. They may continue to brace for collapse, to measure themselves by performance, or to interpret difficulty as a threat to standing—long after standing has been secured.

Faith grows as this realization deepens. Repentance continues as old patterns are exposed as unnecessary and incoherent.

What once felt essential is revealed as survival behavior tied to unstable ground. Over time, life begins to reflect the stability beneath it—not because effort has increased, but because fear has lost its authority.

This does not happen all at once. Not perfectly—but truly.

Alignment deepens. Direction steadies. The logic of the pit loosens its grip as the reality of solid ground becomes increasingly difficult to deny.

Leaving the pit behind is not a dramatic leap. It is a gradual refusal to keep living by rules that no longer apply.

Summary

This chapter has clarified faith and repentance as the visible response to relocation rather than the means of achieving it. Faith brings into visibility what is already true. Repentance is the directional change that follows standing on solid ground.

Faith, properly understood, is a state of existence that acknowledges truth as objectively real with inescapable consequences and in which one's life is ordered accordingly. It does not create reality or secure standing. It recognizes that standing has already been given and begins to live consistently with that fact.

Repentance flows from this recognition. It is the gradual reorientation of life away from the logic of the pit and toward coherence with the ground that now holds. It is not self-condemnation, but movement. Not perfection, but alignment over time.

Neither faith nor repentance earns standing. Both reveal where standing already exists. They are not efforts to escape the pit, but the lived expression of having been placed on the Rock.

Application: Questions of Ground

1. How have you previously understood faith—as effort, agreement, or reliance?

2. In what ways have you treated repentance as punishment rather than reorientation?

3. What behaviors or assumptions still belong to the logic of the pit?

4. How does living as though Christ is Lord differ from trying to prove belief?

5. Where do you feel pressure to earn what has already been given?

6. What might visible alignment with reality look like in ordinary life?

Where to Stand

10

Where Are You Standing?

The Question That Has Been There All Along

This book has not been asking whether you are sincere, moral, thoughtful, or searching. It has not measured effort, intention, or intensity. From the beginning, it has been asking a quieter question—one that cannot be postponed forever.

Where are you standing?

Not where you hope to stand. Not where you intend to stand someday. Not where you believe you should be standing.

But where you are standing now.

This question has been present from the start. It has surfaced whenever sand shifted, whenever weight

217

pressed, whenever guilt or justice or death demanded an answer. Every chapter has returned to it, because every other question depends on it.

Everything else—belief, behavior, intention, and effort —flows from where you are standing.

And no amount of sincerity can substitute for ground.

Two Grounds, One Reality

There are not many kinds of ground.

There are two.

There is sand—unstable, shifting, unable to bear weight. And there is rock—solid, tested, unmoved by pressure or death. Every life is built on one or the other. There is no third option and no neutral place between them.

Standing on sand does not always feel chaotic. It can feel productive, meaningful, even moral. Sand often supports activity for a time. It allows movement, progress, and the appearance of stability. Its failure is not immediate.

But when weight is applied—when guilt presses, when justice demands, when loss or death intrudes— sand always reveals itself. What could be managed collapses. What could be postponed comes due.

Standing on the Rock does not remove struggle or suffering. It does not insulate life from pressure. But it changes what that pressure rests upon. The weight that would crush on sand has already been borne elsewhere. Stability no longer depends on performance, control, or denial.

Scripture presents this distinction not as a spectrum, but as a reality that must eventually be faced.

The difference is not effort. Both houses are built. Both face the storm. The difference is what holds when the storm arrives.

There is one reality—and two grounds on which it can be faced.

"Whosoever heareth these sayings of mine, and doeth them, I will liken him unto a wise man, which built his house upon a rock...

And every one that heareth these sayings of mine, and doeth them not, shall be likened unto a foolish man, which built his house upon the sand."

(Matthew 7:24–27)

What Makes the Difference

The difference between these two grounds is not effort, intelligence, or virtue. It is not religious background, moral success, or sincerity of intent.

219

The difference is **relocation**.

Standing on solid ground is not something you achieve. It is something you receive. You are placed where the weight has already been borne and where judgment has already been faced. Stability is not produced by improvement; it is inherited by placement.

This is why the decisive question is not, "Are you good enough?" That question assumes effort can compensate for unstable ground.

> *"By whom also we have access by faith into this grace wherein we stand."*
>
> *(Romans 5:2)*

The real question is simpler—and more difficult to evade: Are you still trying to stand on ground that cannot hold?

Scripture describes this difference not as a comparison of human ability, but as a matter of position—where one has been set.

Notice the order. Standing is not earned by effort applied upward. Access is given, and standing follows. The ground is entered, not constructed.

Nothing else ultimately explains the difference.

Not dIscipline.

Not insight.

Not resolve.

Only where the weight is being carried.

Why Delay Is Also a Decision

One of the easiest ways to avoid this question is delay.

Not rejection—delay. Not denial—postponement.

Delay feels harmless because it feels passive. It appears to leave options open. But delay does not suspend reality. It leaves a person standing exactly where they already are.

The ground does not wait.

Weight continues to accumulate. Instability continues to press. Time does not neutralize sand; it tests it. What feels tolerable in the moment becomes unmanageable under continued load.

"Today if ye will hear his voice, harden not your hearts."

(Hebrews 3:15)

Standing on sand is not neutral simply because it feels familiar. Familiarity does not strengthen ground. It only dulls awareness of its weakness.

221

Scripture speaks to this dynamic without urgency or threat—simply as recognition of exposure.

Notice what is assumed. The issue is not lack of information, but postponement of alignment. Delay does not preserve possibility; it preserves position.

To delay is not to remain undecided.

It is to continue standing where one already is.

What It Means to Stand on the Rock

To stand on the Rock is not to claim certainty about everything. It is not to possess answers to every question or to feel confident at all times.

Standing does not eliminate mystery. It does not remove weakness. It does not produce constant clarity.

It does something far simpler—and far more decisive.

To stand on the Rock is to stop defending ground that cannot hold.

It is to stop negotiating with instability.

It is to stop acting as though collapse must be managed rather than escaped.

Standing means reliance.

It is choosing to rest the weight of life on what has already been revealed, tested, and proven. It is living in acknowledgment that the decisive question has been settled—not by insight or effort, but by endurance that has already occurred.

Scripture describes this kind of standing not as mastery, but as dependence.

> "The LORD is my rock, and my fortress, and my deliverer."
>
> (Psalm 18:2)

Notice the posture. The Rock is not something to be explained or improved. It is something to be trusted—to bear what the person standing cannot.

Standing on the Rock means living as though Christ truly is Lord.

Not because doing so earns standing,

but because standing makes that way of living coherent.

Once the ground no longer shifts, life no longer has to pretend it does.

No Formula, No Performance

There is no formula to recite here.

No ritual to complete.

No performance to offer.

Standing does not begin with words spoken correctly or actions completed successfully. It begins where pretense ends—where the attempt to manage appearances gives way to acknowledgment of reality.

Faith is not summoned; it is released.

Repentance is not punishment; it is movement away from what no longer holds.

Confession is not an incantation; it is alignment with what is now undeniably true.

None of these add weight to the ground. None of them secure standing.

> "For my yoke is easy, and my burden is light."
>
> (Matthew 11:30)

They simply stop resisting it.

Scripture consistently refuses to frame standing with God as a matter of complexity or performance.

Notice what is absent. There is no technique to master, no threshold to cross, no demon-stration required. What is heavy has already been borne. What remains is not effort, but rest.

Nothing needs to be added. Nothing needs to be proven.

Standing does not begin when something is accomplished.

It begins when something is acknowledged—and allowed to be enough.

The Invitation That Remains

The invitation is simple—but it is not shallow.

You do not need to make the ground solid. You do not need to carry the weight. You do not need to justify yourself.

Those tasks have already been answered—and finished.

What remains is not achievement, but recognition. Not construction, but location. Not effort, but honesty.

You need only to stop standing where standing is impossible—and to stand where life can actually grow.

This is not a leap into uncertainty.

It is a step onto what has already been tested.

The Rock is not fragile.

It does not depend on confidence, understanding, or resolve.

It has already held.

Final Reflection

Take a moment—without pressure, without performance—and consider this honestly:

- Where do you instinctively look for stability?

- What do you rely on when guilt or fear presses in?

- What ground are your choices actually resting on?

These answers matter—not because they determine whether you are accepted, but because they reveal where you are already standing.

A Closing Word

If you are still standing on sand, this book does not condemn you. It tells you the truth. Sand cannot hold —but Rock can.

If you are standing on the Rock, this book does not congratulate you. It reminds you why standing is possible at all.

Either way, reality has been revealed.

The only question left is one you cannot avoid forever:

Where will you stand?

End Notes

Chapter 1 Section 1

1. According to a 2022 survey by the Foundation for Individual Rights and Expression (FIRE), nearly **45%** of Americans say they do not feel free to speak their minds because of the social consequences.

2. A Deloitte study found that **61%** of employees "cover" (hide or downplay) parts of their identity at work to fit in.

3. Pew Research shows that "cross-pressured" individuals (those whose views don't perfectly align with one party) are increasingly rare, as **social pressure** forces people to adopt the full "bundle" of a group's beliefs.

Where to Stand

Further Reading

Some readers may wish to explore questions raised by this book that extend beyond its immediate scope. The following works engage those questions more fully, addressing the broader realities that surround—and secure—the act of standing on solid ground.

The World That Groans

This work examines the deeper fracture beneath human instability: the condition of creation itself. Where Where to Stand focuses on personal location, responsibility, and relocation, The World That Groans moves upstream, tracing the biblical account of a world subjected to disorder through rebellion, corruption, and loss of harmony. It explores why instability is not merely psychological, cultural, or political, but creational—and why the longing for stability is inseparable from the hope of redemption.

Fortress of Justification

Many who step onto solid ground soon ask a further question: how does standing remain secure when guilt resurfaces, accusations return, or failure intrudes again? Fortress of Justification addresses that question by focusing on the biblical doctrine of justification. Rather than treating forgiveness as a feeling or moral achievement, it presents justification as an objective and defended standing before God—

one that does not rest on performance, resilience, or consistency, but on Christ alone.

These and other works can be found at fireproofcommentaries.org

About the Author

James J. Burke is a pastor, writer, and teacher whose work focuses on clarity, moral responsibility, and the recovery of solid ground in an age of instability. He serves as senior pastor of Grace Community Church in Marinette, Wisconsin, where his ministry emphasizes careful exposition of Scripture, pastoral honesty, and the formation of durable Christian faith.

Burke is the founder of Fireproof Commentaries, a writing project devoted to producing theologically serious, accessible works for ordinary readers— especially those who sense that the explanations they have inherited no longer hold. His writing consistently engages questions of identity, justice, guilt, and responsibility, seeking to address them not primarily as cultural problems, but as matters of standing before reality and before God.

He has spent decades working with individuals and congregations navigating disillusionment, moral exhaustion, and spiritual instability, and his writing reflects that pastoral context rather than an academic one. His work is shaped by long attention to Scripture, classical Christian theology, and the lived experience of people trying to stand upright in a shifting world.

James lives in Wisconsin with his wife, Roxanne, and their family.

Where to Stand

Where to Stand